Caring for Ourselves While Caring for Our Elders

caring for ourselves
while caring for our elders

Maren C. Tirabassi

Leanne McCall Tigert

Maria I. Tirabassi

THE PILGRIM PRESS
CLEVELAND

The Pilgrim Press, 700 Prospect Avenue, Cleveland, Ohio 44115-1100
thepilgrimpress.com

© 2007 by Maren C. Tirabassi, Leanne M. Tigert, and Maria I. Tirabassi

Scripture quotations, unless otherwise noted, are from the New Revised Standard Version of the Bible, © 1989 by the Division of Christian Education of the National Council of Churches of Christ in the United States of America and are used by permission. Changes have been made for inclusivity.

11   10   09   08   07   5   4   3   2   1

Library of Congress Cataloging-in-Publication Data

Tirabassi, Maren C.
   Caring for ourselves while caring for our elders / Maren C. Tirabassi, Leanne McCall Tigert, Maria I. Tirabassi.
   p. cm.
   Includes index.
   ISBN 978-0-8298-1717-1
   1. Caregivers—Religious life. 2. Older people—Care. I. Tigert, Leanne McCall, 1957– II. Tirabassi, Maria I., 1983– III. Title.
BV4910.9.T57 2007
259'.3—dc22   2007003052

c o n t e n t s

introduction

But Naomi Isn't Even My Mother
Faith Concerns of Caregivers for Elders

What kind of title is that? Not only is it the title of one of our stories, but it was also the working title for the whole book, because we wanted to remind ourselves, as well as others, that contemporary issues and concerns of caregiving for elders—long-distance management, blended families, past alienations rooted in old prejudices or misunderstandings—are as recent as yesterday's phone call to the church office, senior center, or assisted living facility, and as old as the book of Ruth, where a middle-aged foreign widow accepts residential, financial, and emotional responsibility for her mother-in-law.

There are many people like Ruth—perhaps balancing work and even children with errand running, bill paying, appointment accompanying, Medicare organizing, house selling, emotion steadying, and meaning making for an older family member or for several who live across the street or across the nation. There are many people like Ruth—exhausted and compassionate, courageous in the way that means putting one foot in front of another on the way to some new home and trying to glean little bits of information and hope and spiritual strength. We don't know much about the disciple John's later life, but we do know that Jesus gave him the responsibility to care for his mother Mary. This book is for you, all the "Ruths" and "Johns."

Caring for Ourselves While Caring for Our Elders is organized as a resource for personal reflection or as a discussion starter for a group of people who come together for mutual support in community or church settings.

Following this introduction are twenty-five short chapters that tell stories about elder care situations. These stories were shared with us by some remarkably honest people. The original information has been blended and combined. Sometimes the gender, age, number of siblings, profession or diagnosis has been changed, but never the fears, confusions, doubts, angers, frustrations, satisfactions, or joys. We have tried to share the truth of each story we discovered under its facts. Each story has been paired with a biblical passage that shares some key points of resemblance. Some texts are closer to the stories than others, but the scriptures themselves were chosen as important ones to reflect upon as we seek a faith response, which might be different from a "convenient" response or even a logical response.

In addition to the anecdote, there is a short psychological commentary on the situation, some biblical background for the text, and the heart of this book—questions for discussion or reflection. We hope that these questions will form a bridge between case studies of people you will never know and your own very personal situation. Perhaps only one question will speak to your issues or perhaps you will be in a group where one member feels that every question opens up his or her current dilemma. Perhaps you will want to bring your own questions to the story, the scripture, or the community you will form if you read this as part of a group.

For each chapter there is an "assignment," which is a brief activity for the week—some usually light and nonverbal way to integrate one or more of the issues in the contemporary story or the biblical story. Finally, there is a prayer for those who share some aspect of this situation.

Not everyone's story is included here! If this were a sociology textbook, it could be faulted for having some situations that are similar to each other, while omitting other family paradigms. We realize that by choosing situations accessible to us we have limitations. Maria has particularly worked during this process to include stories from her generation—the teenage and young adult "grand-generation" who may be active caregivers, anxious observers, vocal critics, or victims of the changes in their families.

The final section in the book includes an overview of some of the psychological issues involved in contemporary elder care and a discussion of some overarching biblical themes.

The blessing in this book is not in the stories we gathered and shared, but in the stories we hope will be shared because of them. For universality and completeness we are counting on our readers! There is a threefold purpose to this book:

1. for you to have a chance to tell your own stories, sharing the choices you have made and the feelings you have experienced

2. for you to anticipate the possibilities of what might happen in your situation in the future so that you can discuss and choose a plan using your faith as part of your family strategy

3. for you to share the stories of what has happened in the past and, if necessary, find a way to let them go

Here are two contrasting images of aging taken from scripture. One appears in John 21. Jesus tells Peter that when he becomes old, he will stretch out his hands and someone will fasten a belt around him and take him where he does not want to go. It is perhaps the situation most feared by older people in our society. I can remember my father, who retained liquid as a result of his failing heart, needing to be strapped into a Hoya lift to be moved from chair to bed.

The second image is from the end of Ruth. Naomi's friends congratulate her after the birth of Obed, who is not biologically her grandchild, "He shall be to you a restorer of life and a nourisher of your old age; for your daughter-in-law who loves you, who is more than seven sons, has borne him." I think of a college student volunteer who came to the Alzheimer's unit and read Mitch Albom's *Tuesdays with Morrie* to a gathering of women. What an odd choice, I thought. No, responded my mother. This is someone who is not part of our families but is willing to talk to us about what we are all thinking.

You Ruths and disciple Johns who are reading this book may be looking for ways so that those you care about can avoid being "bound" and experienced being nourished. Often the only way that can happen is for your own ties to be loosened and your own cups to sometimes overflow.

We want to express our deep appreciation. We are grateful to those who have shared their stories and their thoughts—without censoring their not-very-Christian emotions so that our anecdotes could be real rather than perfect. We are grateful to the elders in our lives who made us want to put this resource together in the first place—Russell and Elizabeth Snider, Josephine and Clyde Tirabassi, William and Betty Geoghegan, and Robert and Ruth Ann Tigert. Patience, support, and good humor have characterized our partners, Emily Geoghegan and Donald Tirabassi. Sarah, Rachel, Matt, and Julia have graciously shared our time and attention with this project. The gentle caregivers of Langdon Place of Exeter, New Hampshire, who have supported the Sniders and Tirabassis in many transitions are a model for excellence in professional eldercare. Finally, Kim Martin Sadler, our all-time favorite editor for The Pilgrim Press, has supported—nourished—this book from its initial idea to this conclusion, as well as told us stories of her own family over the last several years. Such sharing is the "precious oil" that the psalmist calls the kinship of faith.

part one

CAREGIVING AT HOME —
AS THINGS BEGIN TO CHANGE

For everything there is a season . . .

ECCLESIASTES 3:1

1 ᕫ Respect and Uncomfortable Truth

Leviticus 19:32; 20:9

Mark is the oldest; Michael next, then Haley and Joshua are twins and the babies. They're a close family, all still living in the same town. Their children go to the same schools, and every week, they get together to have dinner. Their parents, Patricia and James, are content to look across town at their brood from the house in which they raised them. It's a sprawling monstrosity that allowed everyone to have his or her own room growing up, and there are plenty of nooks and crannies for the grandkids. The stairs, however, are steep, with a railing that doesn't go all the way to the top, and last winter James fell and broke his hip.

His recovery has been slow, and, although all four kids are happy to pitch in and help mow the lawn, shovel the snow, and go to the grocery store, it's been hard. Twice now he's tried to take his pills with a nightcap, and Patricia has called, frantic, for one of them to drive them to the hospital.

James laughs off these incidents, but they've deeply shaken his wife. She tries to watch him, but the strain of it is starting to show. He gets angry with her when she hides his liquor. He doesn't like being treated like a child, and she hates treating him that way.

Patricia is also on a daily pill regimen, and, while her cancer is in remission, it left her weak. It's a presence in her life. Her doctor as much as told her it would come back. Cancer kills the people in her family; both of her siblings have already died. She hasn't been the same since she returned from the hospital. She often panics when she has to perform tasks that take her out of the house alone, and she's constantly worrying about the fact that she can't take better care of James on days when his pain gets really bad.

Neither will consider having a nurse come check on them, and they resent the idea that anyone outside of the family would be needed to help. Patricia's brother and sister both had hospice—end-of-life care—and that's what home health care will always be to her. Their children feel guilty for having suggested it, but they all have their own careers and families. The only real arguments they ever seem to have stem from this guilt.

Are we being selfish?

Haley says, yes, but the men disagree. She thinks that by begrudging her parents anything they need, they're setting a poor example for their own children as well as disrespecting the people who cared for them so well. However, she is also the one who is away most often and handles the fewest number of crises.

Is it really too much to ask to spend a weekend away every now and then?

Michael has a condo in the mountains he never gets to use. Haley's work keeps her booked on trips around the country, so she couldn't possibly go away for fun. Joshua would like to start working at camps with his wife in the summer. Mark works from home and never seems to take the vacations he dreams about. As the oldest, he feels he should set an example, but at the same time he doesn't think he can shoulder the weight of this without ongoing help from his brothers and sister.

How can they be angry with us when it feels like we spend every waking moment attending to their needs?

Mark wonders if they're really doing enough and if their parents are at risk staying where they are. He and Joshua think it might be time for their parents to move into a smaller place, but Haley and Michael feel it would be wrong to move them from the only house they've called home since they married. It doesn't seem like it's safe to leave them where they are, but none of them can even bring themselves to discuss this with James and Patricia.

PSYCHOLOGICAL COMMENT

Anger, frustration, and the threat of conflict are often present in families addressing difficult choices with no obvious right or wrong answer. Anger can be a sign of underlying grief, fear, and loss of control.

In the elderly, alcohol use can be an effort to numb these feelings, even in those without a prior history of alcoholism. The dangerous combination of alcohol and prescription medicines is a common situation, especially when some memory loss is involved. Even close families need more skills in difficult conversations in order to make the best decisions under trying circumstances. This is the time that a family therapist or professional care planner might empower people to work cooperatively together to address issues that need tending. In this situation, these issues include James's misuse of alcohol, the shadow that cancer casts, and the potential for burnout of adult children with "sandwich generation" responsibilities.

BIBLICAL BACKGROUND

Leviticus has a bad reputation. Much of it seems boring or antiquated to modern ears and some verses have been taken from the original context and used for "proof-text" attacks (such as those on same-gender couples). In its own context Leviticus was a book of guidelines for worship and living, which actually begins at approximately Exodus 25 and continues through the first ten chapters of Numbers. It was called in early Rabbinic tradition "The Priests' Manual," and is divided into six parts—the Holiness Code, chapters 17–26, being the fifth. In its present form it is a relatively late set of laws with the intention of making the Israelites holy and separate from the practices of their neighbors' religions. Much of chapter 19 complains about the practices of other peoples, such as necromancy and sacred prostitution, but it also contains "Love your neighbor as yourself," (verse 18b), which was adopted from this context by Jesus as the second great commandment (Matt. 12:31 and parallels).

Two verses from Leviticus give us some insight into relationships with elders in the terms of this code. Leviticus 19:32 is significant because it enjoins respect for *all* older people rather than only relatives. This broadening from family loyalty is worth reflection. Leviticus 20:9, which is strictly family oriented, calls for the death penalty (a common punishment for many infractions in this code) for those who curse father or mother. A curser is as culpable as someone doing physical harm! Worth noting in this ancient guideline written from a particularly patriarchal era of Israel's history is the remarkable fact that it is phrased with gender equality—father *or* mother.

QUESTIONS FOR DISCUSSION AND REFLECTION

1. What do you think is "cursing" one's parents in our contemporary culture?

2. In what ways does our contemporary culture respect or "disrespect" elders?

3. Reflect on the level of communication in this story? How could it be improved?

4. Sometimes a house becomes a significant "personality" in a family drama. Have you ever experienced that kind of situation?

ASSIGNMENT: Enjoy an "It's-Not-My-Birthday" Cake

Buy or bake a cake (chocolate is a good idea) for dessert for your family, however you shape family. Put a little candle on the cake for every worry or irritation of the week . . . you don't need to share these aloud. Light them. Instead of making a wish, say a silent prayer, and blow the worries and irritations out. . . . Of course, eat the cake.

PRAYER

Loving God, we are not always at our best, and even the best of us struggles to know what is right and wrong in these times. Help us to use the strength of our love and care for one another to keep us close. Help us talk to each other, rather than about each other. Keep us focused on the truth, remembering that respect comes in many different forms. May we be open to new ways of loving and growing. Amen.

2 ⤳ The *Corban* Scam

Mark 7:9–13

Everybody does it—doesn't make it right," her mother used to say when Diane was a teenager. The choices under discussion were clear-cut—or, at least, they are to Diane now that she has three teenagers of her own. Everybody drinking beer at the barbecue doesn't make it right. Everybody speeding on Jenkins Road doesn't make it right. Everybody looking the other way when athletes cheat doesn't make it right. Diane thinks she remembers similar fiats about joints, necking, and other perils of growing up in the 1970s issued by her parent . . . and it makes her grateful for every fight she doesn't have with her own kids!

Now the issue *is* her parents. For the first time Diane wonders if the "everybody" Pete and Liz are copying isn't just as wrong . . . biblically speaking.

Diane would never have found Mark 7:9–13 except her mind wandered across the page during a Bible study about Jesus walking on the water. She'd been looking forward to that passage because it seemed like walking on water is what it would take to keep her life afloat. Fifty this year, Diane works thirty-seven hours a week at a local bookstore and edits manuscripts freelance for a couple of small publishers. Gill is a musician. When they divorced five years ago, she expected little financial help from him, and she hasn't been disappointed. She *had* expected he at least would stay in the state so he could have some kind of relationship with his three children. She was stunned when he and Melissa produced baby number four. The last person in the world . . .

Diane can hold things together, but college will be the challenge—Lindsey is a junior with pre-med dreams; Katelyn is a sophomore who wants to be a public defender (thus, law school) and Ty, still in the eighth grade, is hoping for a culinary institute—not, to Diane's surprise, an inexpensive form of higher education. She remembers that Gill and she had the brilliant idea to have children close enough to be "friends." Great!

So when Diane's folks, Pete and Liz, attended a retirement seminar and started gifting and shifting money into the kids' names, then seeing a lawyer to "protect" Diane and her sister Marty's legacy, it seemed a fantastic idea, a heaven-sent reward for all the hard work and worrying they'd all done. Pete and Liz are both eighty-two. Liz is in remission from breast cancer. Pete has an odd way of casting around too long for the right word, and he gets them lost in streets they know perfectly well.

Marty and Gary don't have kids so they don't really care about any "legacy," but Diane has grown accustomed to counting on it—even counting it, and she knows that assisted living or nursing home care would drain everything. Even though she knows she isn't "entitled" to help, it means a lot that she is getting it. She doesn't want her kids to have to settle—they should be able to achieve their educational aspirations without constantly worrying about the impact on the rest of the family. If their grandparents are willing to provide . . . Diane doesn't like to think about it too hard, but she has her doubts.

Corban. She asked her pastor. It's the Hebrew word for money set aside so that it can't be used to support a mother or father. Isn't that just exactly what they are doing—setting up *corban*, a legitimate hiding place so their savings won't be spent for their own care? Diane wants desperately to believe this is something other than what it seems. Are they cheating the government? Cheating Lindsey, Katelyn, and Ty's generation ultimately . . . in general? But Diane doesn't think she is ready to sacrifice her own children's college education to some overactive scruples. Why should they suffer? Why should they be buried in loans until they're fifty? The solution is there at hand. What's so wrong with taking advantage of the system? The people who do it get ahead. It wouldn't make a difference—except to them. Everybody does it.

PSYCHOLOGICAL COMMENT

Money is a "taboo topic" for many families—as off limits as sex and politics. The way that families share, hoard, speak of, or maintain secrecy around money is often indicative of their level of anxiety or the health of psychological boundaries. How money is controlled and distributed speaks to the negation of power within relationships. If this family had been able to speak more openly and directly about money, some of the worry and fear Diane feels might be addressed more effectively, and they could work together for each other's benefit.

BIBLICAL BACKGROUND

The Pharisees or, in Hebrew, "separate ones," tried to renew Judaism by strict regulations for the Sabbath, fasting and food purity. They adhered to not only the laws of Moses but the wider code of Mishnah and Talmud. Pharisees had no religious professional status and worked at secular jobs. They were popular with most common people because they established synagogues and schools. Unlike most other Jewish groups of the time, they believed in resurrection. The conflict of the early Christian church with the group that dominated Judaism after the destruction of the Temple certainly influenced the way the gospel writers reported on Jesus' relationship with them. In many regards his message of reform was similar to theirs.

Jesus' conflict with the Pharisees focused on their strictness and lack of compassion in applying their regulations. Mark 7 begins with Pharisees criticizing Jesus' failure to wash his hands with ritual correctness. He returned the challenge by pointing out the disparity between the much more central commandment to honor parents and the allowance for *corban*—financial resources which, by being symbolically offered to God, became available for personal use but were not available to care for relatives in their old age. He accused the Pharisees of hygiene and hypocrisy!

QUESTIONS FOR DISCUSSION AND REFLECTION

1. Is protecting assets and "spending down" to Medicaid a contemporary form of *corban*?

2. How does your family communicate about money? Can you imagine talking openly about money as a shared resource to benefit all?

3. Should our country be moving towards privately or publicly funded eldercare?

4. Jesus often critiqued Pharisees for putting heavy burdens on people who lived on the margins. Do you empathize with Diane's needs?

ASSIGNMENT: Waste Money

Yes. Take twenty dollars and spend the week figuring out how to waste it . . . or spend it on frivolous or unnecessary things. You may want to give some away—to a panhandler or a cause you have never participated in. You may want to indulge in some small pleasure for yourself, someone you love, or someone you don't know. You may want a souvenir of the experience (something pretty tacky). You might even want to burn a dollar or two or use it for origami. Let the ways you use this money help you reflect on financial worries you have or ways in which money has gained an unnatural hold on you.

PRAYER

O God of great abundance, so often we focus on the scarcity of supplies rather than the greatness of your gifts. Empower us to be open with one another about our needs and wants. Enable us to give and share, trusting your care for us as individuals and families. May we be so bold as to speak the truth of economic injustice in our country, and advocate for those least able to care for themselves. Amen.

3 ⤳ If It's a Commandment, It Must Not Be Natural

Exodus 20:12

My family is the one people always stare at. I'm used to it—it's been this way my whole life—it's something you accept because family is family, and you love them, regardless of anything. My father is white and my mother is black. I have one white sister, two black sisters, and a brother who, like me, is a mix . . . or a blend.

When I was younger, I didn't understand what the big deal was, but I always knew that a big deal existed. It sort of split up the family. My uncle won't come see us anymore, because he thinks my mom lets herself be "dominated." If he came to our house, he would see right away that he was wrong. Our home has the most and the best love of any place I've ever been.

I never met my dad's parents. They died before I was even born, and my dad doesn't talk much about them. I just know that they were really sick and that he had to take care of them at their house after he was divorced. My sister, Louisa, says he did a good job taking care of them without forgetting about her.

My mom's mom died, too, only a month ago. She used to come watch us when we were little. She was a really great cook, and Mom says I take after her. She used to bring her boyfriend too. My sister Margaret says, "boyfriend—right!" but I thought Walter was nice. He used to take all five of us to the movies; he'd always pick one that we would all like and buy us popcorn.

He's been spending a lot of time at our house since Grandma El died. My dad says he doesn't have any family of his own—no kids or cousins or anything—and that Grandma was the only person in his life. I don't think my parents are all that happy he's here. They're trying to be nice, but my mom's having a hard time. I know she's just really sad and seeing him every day makes it more real, but I think she and Dad could be more understanding. Walter doesn't have anywhere else to go, and it cheers him up to spend time with us kids.

My sister Nina says he's making himself a "nuisance" hanging around the way he is, but she doesn't know what she's talking about. She's fourteen, and she thinks she understands everything, but she really doesn't. If she did, she would know that he's feeling even worse than any of us because when he goes home at night, there's nobody to talk to or laugh with. He doesn't have any way of forgetting about Grandma El being gone. Also, I heard my mom and dad talking about how much the funeral cost, how he paid for it, because they didn't have life insurance or anything, and how Walter probably doesn't have anything but Social Security. Dad said that was why they didn't get married. I don't think my folks want him to move in here. It's pretty crowded already, with the seven of us, and only four bedrooms; we all share already, and we'd have to share even more, but maybe it would be okay.

That probably won't happen though. Nobody seems to think of Walter as family . . . at least not now. Two months ago, I don't think anyone would have said he wasn't! When it comes to helping him out, I guess it seems like more trouble than he's worth. Margaret says I just don't understand about "finances" and what's "appropriate," but I do. I know all about that stuff, and I still think it's wrong to turn someone away, even if he's not family—even if he's just a friend. He always liked our family better than some of our own flesh and blood, and I think that should count for something.

PSYCHOLOGICAL COMMENT

The definition of "family" is rapidly changing in our society. As our understanding of marriage and parenting shifts, so does our experience of caring for elders. Family can be understood as legal status, or as relational responsibility. More people are choosing for themselves whom they define as "family" in their lives. This, in turn, creates connections and loyalties far different from the legal categories of responsible next-of-kin. After a death, those who remain may find that their definitions are challenged.

If families (however defined) cannot talk about these relationships and honor one another's choices before a crisis emerges, then it becomes much more difficult to honor one another's wishes in the moment. Old family structures may not be adequate to care for the present-day needs of blended families. We need to communicate with one another about whom we love and how we want people to treat our families of choice. We must talk about our fears and limitations as we are pushed toward ever broadening and deepening relationships. Love is constantly creating new possibilities for us all.

BIBLICAL BACKGROUND

The Ten Commandments' function in Exodus and Deuteronomy is less to list strictures and prohibitions than to define a relationship between the Hebrew people, recently liberated from Egypt, and their God. It followed the format of a treaty with a secular ruler, which always opened with a prologue describing the obligation. The Ten Commandments were counted in slightly variant ways by different texts and traditions, but, in each case, honor or respect for mother and father appeared as the first commandment about human interaction and, as noted by the writer of the letter to the Ephesians (Eph. 6:2b–3), it is the commandment with an attached promise—"so that your days will be long" or "so that it will go well with you" in the land. Jesus cited this commandment as one of the essential ones for eternal life in the story of the rich young ruler (Matt. 19:19 and parallels).

QUESTIONS FOR DISCUSSION AND REFLECTION

1. If honoring parents must be listed with the laws, does that imply that it is not a natural human instinct?

2. In your experience, do people who care for parents actually receive this promise of long life and well-being?

3. What does "honor" mean, and can it vary in different situations?

4. Walter has no biological relationship to the family in this story. Whom do you consider "family" in your life? Is this

definition based upon legal ties, blood, behavior, choice, intention, or something else?

5. Can you imagine a way that this family might have proactively addressed the stress that they were experiencing surrounding the death of Grandma El?

ASSIGNMENT: Write a Letter

You probably have a wide range of feelings about your parents, step-parents or grandparents. Today, however, reflect on one non-relative you want to honor. Think about a teacher, coach, pastor, counselor, neighbor, or older friend who helped to shape your life and write a letter of appreciation and thanks. Send it, if the person is still living. Send it to someone dear to that person, if he or she has died.

PRAYER

God of foster-father Joseph, in-law-grandma Naomi, Uncle Mordecai, stepmothers Rachel and Leah, surrogate Hagar, the young princess who adopted Moses, and the old apostle who adopted Onesimus—we thank you for the amazing shapes and complicated connections of our families. Help us to experience the blends and the bonds as blessings and to sustain with your grace all who are isolated from the welcome that makes a family out of any situation. Amen.

4 ❧ Promises, Promises

Genesis 46–50, especially 47: 29–31 and 48:8–20

When Tony was honest with himself, he knew that his father had always been a petty tyrant, a little Caesar. And now, here he was, reclining like a roman senator, eating his bunches of grapes, served by his slaves and entertained by gladiatorial combat in his family.

His mother, Angela, never seemed to mind: "When Frank's happy, everybody's happy." She loved to cook his favorite meals, socialize with his colleagues, press his shirts. When she went to help her sister after a difficult childbirth, she bought ten new shirts, then washed and pressed them so Frank wouldn't be inconvenienced. If Frank were thwarted, the anger sat like a snow bank in the living room . . . for a long time. Nothing was ever forgotten.

In high school Tony forgot to pick up Rose from her flute lesson and his dad was called away from a cocktail party. The immediate punishment was shaming—the slap in front of all his friends—and the ongoing punishment extreme—he couldn't use the car for his entire junior year. At fifty-two, Tony still hears Frank say to a casual acquaintance with a disarming laugh, "Oh, don't ask Tony, he's unreliable. Once he . . ."

"Your dad's just teasing you," Angela would excuse him and, because in public Frank was full of fun and stories, generous with his money and spoiling his grandchildren, the neighbors and friends from church told Tony over and over again how lucky he was.

Some of the time Tony agreed. His father didn't drink, gamble, or cheat on Angela. He was there for Sunday dinners, and heaven help the child who made other plans. He footed the bill for an elegant reception hall for Tony and Carla's daughter Kate and then—

with a big surprise kiss from Grandpa—he paid for her wedding gown, too. But when her older sister Jennifer wanted something different—a state park lodge with no alcohol, a gathering of contemporaries, a justice of the peace, and a turquoise dress, Frank became so angry he didn't even attend. "What—my granddaughter can't wear white? She's not a virgin?" Jennifer didn't care about any money, she just wanted her grandpa to come to her wedding, but, even when Tony pleaded, Frank didn't reconsider.

When Frank turned sixty-five, Angela threw a big party for friends and family (except Jennifer, Aaron, and baby Livy). After all the toasts Frank took them aside—Angela, Tony, Terry, and Rose, with Tony's wife Carla and Rose's husband Dave. (Jack didn't count because he was Terry's second husband.) Frank made them all promise they would never put him in a nursing home. Never.

Never turned out to be a long time. Frank had cancer for six years. He went to bed and Angela waited on him—up and down the stairs with her bad knees. Hospice was brought in and Frank loved the daily visits of nurses, aides, and chaplain. But the burden fell on his wife—coming to the sharp voice on the baby monitor, tempting his picky appetite. Years passed. Hospice stayed, hating to leave the family, although it was hard to justify the extended care. Angela didn't sleep. Frank would call her at night for a glass of water although he easily walked to the bathroom. Carla helped. She came over so Angela could go out to dinner with Rose. Tony was glad his wife was a social worker and Frank's whining rolled past her.

Three months ago Angela was hospitalized with a flu, which turned into pneumonia. Frank spent two weeks in respite care at a beautiful nearby assisted living facility. Carla, with her agency contacts, had arranged it, but, now that Frank was home, her part in this "humiliation" meant that she wasn't welcome at his home. Angela, white as a ghost, was making smoothies and toast and two morning bowls of cereal that had too much milk. "Get me another bowl and don't drown it."

Tony expected that hospice would reevaluate and drop this five-year client . . . or his mother would die. He got together with his sisters and their partners. "We've got to do something." Rose answered, "But we promised." He agreed with her. Terry said, "It's too late . . . way too late." He agreed with her, too.

PSYCHOLOGICAL COMMENT

Families with unhealthy patterns in earlier stages of life often have similar problems when dealing with elder care. In this family, behaviors such as emotional cutoffs (not talking with someone you feel has wronged you), compliance/codependence towards a powerful and controlling man, and fear of confrontation are evident.

Another common pattern is the assumption that placing someone in an assisted living situation when he or she can no longer healthfully be cared for at home is a signal that the person is no longer loved. However, often keeping someone at home means turning the home into an institution itself, creating in the living room what people are trying to avoid in the health care facility.

BIBLICAL BACKGROUND

Jacob made Joseph swear to bring his bones to Machpelah rather than burying him in Egypt. Joseph went to great trouble to embalm his father and take him with all the adults in the family back to Canaan.

In the second highlighted section, it's apparent that Jacob adopted Joseph's two boys as his own. The cultural expectation was that the firstborn child would receive all or the largest share of the legacy. Jacob himself was a younger twin who had tricked his brother Esau out of both inheritance and blessing, and his favoritism with Joseph nearly cost this younger son his life when his jealous brothers first put him in a well and then sold him into slavery. His behavior pattern was family-splitting long before he was asked to bless Manasseh and Ephraim.

QUESTIONS FOR DISCUSSION AND REFLECTION

1. Do you have promises you have made in your life that call now for reevaluation? Is the keeping of promises *always* a Christian value?

2. How can this family use this moment in their life together to change very old patterns?

3. Joseph is angry with Jacob for his uneven treatment of his grandchildren. Tony's story mirrors that. It is a cliché in our culture that the relationship between grandparents and grandchildren is always wonderful. When that isn't true, what can a member of the generation "in between" do to help?

4. If Angela has always accepted this abusive relationship, should her children let it continue or protect her? Who should decide?

5. How can a family keep from institutionalizing the home in the effort to care?

ASSIGNMENT: Draw a Cartoon

Is your parent driving you crazy? Has that person always been difficult? Or is there perhaps a doctor, an administrator, a sibling, or a spouse with whom you are angry, but to whom you must relate? Draw a cartoon of this person. (Feel free to insert conversation balloons, which might say "Gimme, Gimme!" or to exaggerate physical characteristics.) Your cartoon can be savage, but it *must* be funny. Have a good laugh and then *throw it away*.

PRAYER

Holy One, you call us to love and honor, care for, and cherish those to whom we are closest. Yet, sometimes it is too hard. We just cannot see how it can be done. Help us to confront one another with love, to support one another without sacrificing ourselves, and to trust your Spirit to guide and give, even when we have given all. Amen.

part two

CAREGIVING FOR ELDERS IN THE HOME

So your days will be long in the land . . .

EXODUS 20:12

5 A Spirit of Power and Love and Self-Discipline

2 Timothy 1:3–7

Annie spent every summer with her grandmother until she was sixteen. She and her Grandma Ruth picked strawberries in the fields behind her house, caught frogs and threw them back, and went through every thrift store in the area looking for the best bargains. When she was old enough to use the stove, Annie and her grandmother learned how to bake together. Ruth made a gardener out of her. School vacations were eagerly anticipated, and Annie's mother had always appreciated the time to herself.

A few months after Annie turned sixteen, however, her mother passed away. Annie had to step up and help take care of her younger brother so her father could work, and she had less and less time to spend on Ruth's farm. As college came and went, Annie was drawn into the whirlwind of activities, and she spent her free time working to pay off loans. She married her high school sweetheart three months after they received their degrees, and they moved south for his job.

As the years pass, Annie thinks more and more of those summers. Unable to have children, she often looks back at how happy the two of them were and wishes she had grandmothering of her own to look forward to. When her father died, she realized there was no one to watch over Ruth. Annie's brother has a large family and no extra room; besides, he never spent much time with his grandmother and is more interested in doing the legwork to find some sort of nursing home for her.

Annie takes a week to visit Ruth and quickly realizes she's in remarkably good shape for eighty. She's healthy, and there's no real need for medical assistance. She is lonely, though, and Ruth calls

Annie more often after she returns home. In a matter of months, both women recognize that their relationship is as good as, if not better than, it was, and it fills both of them in a way they'd never considered possible. The difference in their ages seems less important than the similarity of interests. Annie has stopped thinking so much about having kids. Instead she's planning ways to be an interesting aunt to her nephews. She can leave a legacy in them.

Annie knows she and Jason have the room to move Ruth in with them. However, he is not willing to disrupt the life they've established. He's grateful that this friendship has pushed his wife away from the danger of depression, but it doesn't seem like that change should mean he has to accept responsibility for another person. For him, discovering that they wouldn't ever have children meant coming to terms with the pros, as well as the cons. A big "pro" was the freedom they would have.

Now, whenever the topic is broached, he begins right in on the lack of privacy they'd have and the burden it would be to help an "old woman" find friends in a new neighborhood. He doesn't want to be responsible for her, and he feels that they have enough problems without taking on one more. Even though Annie tries to tell him about the summers by the lake, he can't understand why she would want her family any closer than they already are. He had a miserable childhood, often left alone while his parents worked. When they did get together with his extended family, his parents treated it as a burden to be endured. The idea that such a burden could enter into their home indefinitely is too much for him to face.

The resulting arguments leave both of them exhausted, and Annie doesn't see an easy solution. If she pushes the issue, Jason may not be able to handle it. She's afraid he might even decide to leave if they can't agree, but she doesn't think it's right to abandon a wonderful woman who is her own flesh and blood. For Annie, it's starting to feel like there's no solution, no way to show both her husband and her grandmother how much she loves them.

PSYCHOLOGICAL COMMENT

No matter how many years pass, the roles that we play in our families of origin rarely change on their own. More often, without introspection and a willingness to grow, patterns of interaction persist. In this story, Annie continues to play the role of the caretaker. She began when her mother died by taking care of her younger brother, and she is continuing by believing she should shoulder the burden of her grandmother's care. Often in families like this it is hard to share responsibilities. Sometimes we can act as if no one else can help—and then they don't. At the same time, Annie's husband describes his childhood as "miserable." He exemplifies what many of us experience—the inability to move beyond our own experience and beliefs in the hope that things might be different.

BIBLICAL BACKGROUND

The three Pastoral Letters (1 and 2 Timothy and Titus) were probably not written by Paul himself. They do come from a mentor in ministry to a young leader in the church. Second Timothy may contain fragments from genuine Pauline letters. The common practice of pseudonymous authorship—assigning authorship to a respected writer—was not dishonest by the cultural standards of the time, but rather a way of honoring and preserving an earlier apostle's work.

Timothy was from Lystra in Asia Minor, the son of a Greek father and a Jewish mother who became a Christian. Timothy is mentioned as Paul's companion in Acts and in Paul's letters to Rome, Corinth, and to the slave owner Philemon. In this letter (whatever the authorship) Timothy's mother and grandmother were lifted up as models of faith. A Christian upbringing, as well as a dramatic conversion, can be the path to faith. The writer also underlined a person's ability to "rekindle" faith that had been banked or even snuffed out by experiences. The author, who was writing from jail, encouraged all young adults to express gratitude to their families and carry on their values in spite of difficulties. Not all of us have a Lois or Eunice in our family—but all of us know one.

QUESTIONS FOR DISCUSSION AND REFLECTION

1. How have differences in family background and experience affected elder care decisions in your life?

2. Have you observed or experienced marital stress because of family issues? How was it resolved? Sometimes marital stress "reappears" as situations change. Are there strategies for ongoing communication?

3. Could physically and mentally competent Ruth be included in this decision-making process? What are some suggestions to facilitate this?

4. What makes a grandparent/grandchild relationship precious? How is it different from a parent/child relationship?

ASSIGNMENT: Do a "Mini" Oral History

Take a tape recorder and visit an older person. Focus on a holiday that is coming up soon—Thanksgiving, Christmas, Valentine's Day, Easter, even the Fourth of July or "summer vacation." A birthday would work as well. Interview the person about memories related to this occasion. Transcribe the tape and make a story you can share. (It can be shaped as a story for a grandchild.) A full memoir is a daunting project—these vignettes can be treasures.

PRAYER

Creator of life, the world is ever changing. May we not be stagnant—stuck in old patterns and roles. Help us to let others help us, to let others know our thoughts, worries, feelings. Help us to risk honesty, vulnerability, hope. May we not be timid in spirit, but move forward together in love, power, and self-control. Amen.

6 ⁀ *No Me Abandones*

Psalm 71

When I got home from work, I called my sister Nina to see if Mama had gotten in safely.

"She's settled, *si*, but she was pretty upset when she got in," she told me. "What were you two talking about this morning?"

"You don't want to know," I said, as I sprinkled fish food into the tank. I could hear Nina talking to somebody in a low voice. "Who's there with you?"

"Marco. He says, 'Tell her to stop bringing up nursing homes right before you send her here.'"

"What's he doing there?" I asked, wracking my brain for my brother's work schedule.

"The band's playing a gig in St. Paul tonight, so he stopped in for free food."

"Well, tell him '*Hola, hermanito*.'" I listened to her relay the greeting. A minute later, the line clicked.

"Penelope? You there?" I heard my little brother's baritone.

"*Si.*"

"Why'd you have to get Mama all *agitada*? She was furious the whole drive home, and now she's *enfurruñada* in her room," he said.

"Because *you* told me to bring it up. *You* told me that somebody had to talk to her, and since I was the oldest, it was my job to crush her poor little *corazón*," I replied.

"Well, you did a good job," he said gruffly.

"Why did you tell her to do that?" Nina interjected, "I thought we agreed to wait it out. If she gets sick, then we bring up the possibility of, you know, elder care. Not before though—I can't believe you brought it up out of the blue. She must be *desolada*."

"I barely even got to say anything," I said. "She just kept shushing me."

"What do you mean?" Marco said.

"Every time I tried to tell her about the options she has, she . . . started to call on the Virgin. I thought she was going to bring out her rosary right in the airport."

Nina said, "I don't know why you're surprised. You know she doesn't want to discuss it . . . and in public!"

"*Lo siento,*" I said, "but what did you want me to do? We all agreed we didn't want to keep moving her around. The monthly rotation was supposed to be a temporary solution, and it's been three years. We need to figure something else out."

"Maybe not, though," Nina said. "If we were in Puerto Rico . . ."

"We're not," Marco said bluntly. He had less tolerance for Nina's backpedaling than I did. "If she wanted us to grow up like that, she should have stayed there. Then we could live all together with our wives and husbands and babies."

"You have no *respeto,*" Nina replied. "Mama's just upset because . . . she has different expectations."

"I think she's *asustada* . . ." I added. "Her English has been getting worse this last year, and she knows it. I don't think she wants us to leave her someplace where nobody speaks Spanish. How would she communicate with the nurses and aides?"

"I can't believe this," he said. "I can't believe you're both making excuses. I thought we were in this together, and now it sounds like I'm the only one committed to making a decision that will eliminate a huge amount of stress from all our lives."

"There's more to it than that," Nina argued. "She's not just a problem. She's a human being."

"Not to mention our *madre!* " I said.

"Still, I thought we were agreed—assisted living would be much better for her than living out of a suitcase in our homes," he said. "Lope, you were the one who opened the can of worms—now you're giving up?"

"*No le dije nada.* I would love to figure something out, but I just don't know how to bring it up. How do we tell her what she doesn't want to hear?"

PSYCHOLOGICAL COMMENT

This story provides another example of the significance of the role of culture in the caretaking of elders, in this case traditional Latino culture. It shows the difficulty between siblings, as well as the conflicting expectations between the generations. By trying to honor their mother's wishes, Nina, Marco, and Lope are finding themselves struggling with limited resources and abilities, as well as their own frustrations of living with differing cultural and social expectations.

In Puerto Rico, they might all be living close together in a neighborhood that spoke their mother's primary language and held a common cultural belief about how she should and could be cared for. However, by living in different cities in the continental United States, they face a very different reality. Negotiating intergenerationally and cross-culturally demands great flexibility, communication skills, and empathy.

BIBLICAL BACKGROUND

Contemporary readers are often disturbed by the mention of "enemies," "the wicked," and "hateful" or "violent" people in the Psalms and the desire by the writers for a justice that sounds perilously close to revenge. Enemies include those who make false accusations or gloat over and take advantage of misfortune, as well as more obvious political enemies. The Psalms claim that God and humans both have enemies and the division between them is often thin.

Like most laments, Psalm 71 puts suffering in the context of a promise of celebration when the suffering has ended. It sounds to modern ears like a bribe—it also sounds uncomfortably like our own prayer lives! This aged worshipper prayed for deliverance from personal enemies and pledged that he or she would use musical talents to share the deliverance, not only in the Temple, but with future generations. Earlier experiences of rescue and comfort are cited—the relationship with God stretched back through childhood to the uterine months before birth. This throws into contrast the complaints about losses inherent in aging in verses 9 and 18. The writer sought consistency in God's favor throughout life. The imagery of protection—rock and fortress—were familiar to early singers and readers. Common to the geography they knew, these symbols of strength were often used metaphorically.

QUESTIONS FOR DISCUSSION AND REFLECTION

1. Can the well-meaning plans of family feel like the attack of enemies?

2. How do isolating limitations, such as loss of English, hearing, vision, or mobility throw a person on the more narrow resources of family?

3. What is your own family cultural heritage? How does it affect the role of elders and elder care? Do you find yourself or others you love having to negotiate differing expectations due to racial, economic, gender, sexual orientation, or geographical differences?

4. The "rotation" caregiving model is less popular than it once was. List advantages and disadvantages of the system.

ASSIGNMENT: Pack a Suitcase

Fill a suitcase for a weeklong trip, as if you were going on vacation, a visit, or a business trip. Put in necessities and some frivolous things as well . . . that paperback mystery. Make sure you can shut the suitcase. Do you feel excitement or dread? Pray for the various kinds of people who are living out of suitcases this week. Try to live out of the suitcase for the next couple days and make notes of your feelings.

PRAYER

O Holy One, we know you across our many different ways, ages, tongues, and races. Though we are different and unique, you are the same; and in your sameness you call us to love one another as we have been loved by you, and as we love ourselves. Help us, O God, and heal our divisions. Empower us to work together creatively in our families and faith communities to care for all who have need. Amen.

7 ⪋ All That Is Mine Is Yours . . .

Luke 15:25–32

How long are they going to stay?" Marshall hissed, when my mother and stepfather finally went upstairs to take a nap. I continued to fold clothes, as though I hadn't heard the question. "They brought more than one suitcase," he muttered. "That means, what, a week? Two? Please say it's not more than two."

"I don't know. Maybe," I said. "We haven't talked about it yet."

"No," he gestured first at himself, then at me, "*we* haven't talked about it yet."

"Don't you think you're being a little unreasonable? They have nowhere to go—there's no money left!"

"And whose fault is that?"

"Shush! They'll hear us."

"I don't care. Look, your mother and stepfather fell for that land scam in Florida and lost all their money—*and* any money you might have inherited some day."

"Lots of people fell for it. They're only guilty of being gullible. Those people prey on the elderly."

"I'll buy that. But most old people cut their losses. I'm going to make a wild guess that only *your* stepfather took what they had left to Vegas to win back their nest egg and then lost everything at the tables."

"It probably wasn't very smart."

"Smart? It was criminal. Now you're supposed to bail them out."

"It's my mother."

Marshall sighed. "You're not guilt tripping me into this. He's not staying. If she wanted to leave him . . ."

I dropped the basket on the floor. "And what if *I* say they are staying? Do you really think you can just set down laws? It doesn't work that way."

"Well, what makes you think you can make a unilateral decision that they stay? How is that more fair?"

"This is ridiculous. You're acting like a child," I said. I turned and started for the stairs. He grabbed my arm and pulled me into the living room, out of carshot of the guest bedroom.

"We just got the kids out of the house. I don't even want to take care of a cat—much less a sixty-eight-year-old couple. They should go out and find jobs again. They are young. They wasted their money—they don't deserve retirement!" Marshall said. "We should be saving for *ours!*"

"Besides, Marshall, how much trouble can they be? We'll put a television up there—they'll be fine. They'll make their own friends."

"Are you kidding me? You think they're going to stare at the boob tube for ten hours a day? Who's going to take them to the doctor? What about visiting friends? They are going to be borrowing our car. It's like having teenagers."

"They'll buy a new car, I'm sure."

"Who will pay for the insurance? Hell, who will pay for a new *car?*"

"We can figure it all out," I said stubbornly. "I'm not just going to abandon them to a homeless shelter. They do have their Social Security coming in."

"I'm sure Foxwoods Casino will be glad to know it!"

"How dare you!"

"OK, so maybe that's a little harsh. Listen, we could help them find a place. People do get old without savings. I know subsidized senior housing isn't their . . . class or expectation, but they sure qualify. If that's what they can afford, that's where they should be. They can stay here while they're on some waiting lists."

"It's not right. Family should take care of family. That's how it used to be done. I don't see why we can't try."

He sat down beside me. "I'm not saying we can't try . . . but they could live for twenty-five more years. I mean, I *hope* they live for twenty-five years, but not under *our* roof. They need something of their own, something independent. We would be making old people out of them. They'd hate owing us."

"*Your* roof is what you mean, right? My mother and her gambling husband under *your* roof, spending *your* money, eating *your* food! You would hate it that they owed *you* money."

"I'm only saying it because I think it's the wrong choice for them."

"And for you," I said.

"And for *us*."

PSYCHOLOGICAL COMMENT

The dynamic of loyalty within families can create very difficult conflicts for many. Often, spouses experience conflicting loyalties between their different families of origin, or between parents and children. This story clearly shows the conflict that someone can feel when trying to care for parents while maintaining the intimacy and commitment of marriage; it adds to the other concerns the dimension of financial mismanagement. In fact, money issues make the situation explosive. The main character in the story feels pulled between the expectations of her mother, her husband, and herself. To some degree, she must choose whom she will please, and whom she will disappoint. Expectations, beliefs, and needs all enter into decisions for caretaking. Family members can help one another by talking together about each of these, and then creatively planning ways to support everyone as much as possible.

BIBLICAL BACKGROUND

In the fifteenth chapter of Luke, Jesus addressed three parables to two audiences—the self-righteous scribes/Pharisees and the tax collectors/sinners. Their responses are unrecorded, but they would have been quite different.

After the metaphor of God as shepherd searching for one lost sheep and God as housewife hunting for one lost coin, the parable, usually called the parable of the prodigal son, portrays a younger son who asked his father to "play dead" by dividing his property between his two children. The younger son's share would have been significantly smaller than his older sibling, who actually would have become the owner of the farm. When the younger son lost his legacy in wild living and descended to feeding pigs—a profession offensive to Jews—he rehearsed an apology and returned to his home. However, his father preempted the speech, dressed him in sandals, which signified that he was not considered a slave, and gave him a ring, which sealed his high status.

Coming in from the fields, the older son heard the welcome home party and refused to enter and "reward" his brother's wasteful behavior. The father confirmed that, indeed, the older son owned everything, but that they should celebrate the return of the prodigal as if he had been dead. Jesus concluded the story by leaving his audiences to decide how the older brother would respond to the father's plea. We are left in the same not very comfortable position.

QUESTIONS FOR DISCUSSION AND REFLECTION

1. If you were to cast yourself in the prodigal son story, what role would you play?

2. Does the fact that the contemporary story has a "prodigal" member of the older generation change your perspective?

3. What are the loyalty conflicts you see in this story? Do you have similar conflicts of loyalty within your own family?

4. Can you imagine some creative possibilities for a successful resolution to the problems in this family? What can families do to prevent this kind of situation?

ASSIGNMENT: Give Away

You may want to look up the First Nation/Native American practice of the giveaway or simply find ways this week to offer some of your possessions to others. Don't buy new presents for friends and family. What might you "leave to someone" after your death? Give it now—a piece of jewelry, a favorite book, a household decoration or piece of furniture.

PRAYER

God, when we are tempted to contrast our good decisions with the unwise ones of others, forgive us. When we feel like money is a real thing that belongs to us, forgive us. When we talk at cross purposes with those we love because we are so sure we are right, forgive us. When family situations surprise us into showing our mean side and then we get defensive, forgive us. May your forgiveness open a quiet space in which all our concerns shrink into perspective, and may our creative problem solving grow in proportion to our need. Amen.

8 ⫘ Is Everybody Happy?

Psalm 128

My father-in-law lives with us. He had a stroke a few months ago, and now he's living in the guest bedroom. This is about as much fun as it sounds. I don't think I'm a cold or heartless person at all, it's just exhausting to be responsible for this man's well-being twenty-four hours a day. And the fact is that I married an older man so his father is the age of my grandfather and doesn't have the good health or the common sense that my own Poppi does.

Granted, I have a fifteen-year-old daughter, which puts me at responsibility central. She's on her way out of the house, and he's on his way to bed-bound. I get excited about her milestones, and all the new things she's accomplishing. Even when I'm exasperated at some foolish "Mom, everyone does it" and have to ground her, I know she is learning something. With him, there's no learning curve. There's no optimism or growth. He is unlearning what he used to know and for him the end won't be graduation.

I feel bad thinking these things, and I feel even worse when I say them aloud, but I'm so tired. Last week, I got into a huge fight with my husband about whether or not his dad should be allowed to keep the keys to his pickup. My husband thinks yes, so he gave him a ring of keys to do with as he likes; unfortunately, what my father-in-law likes to do is drive off without telling anyone where he's going. When he shows up hours later, disoriented and afraid, I'm the one who's been calling around the neighborhood to find out if anyone has seen him.

Anyway, my mother comes over every morning to be with him, and I'm around all afternoon and evening. Either of us would be more than happy to take him out for errands or to visit friends. When he drives, he endangers his own life and the lives of others on the road.

Yesterday I decided I would just take the keys and keep them, and if my father-in-law needs something, we can go out together. I haven't told Bill that I've done this, but I really think it's for the best.

So why do I feel so bad? I'm lying to my husband, and, if I weren't, I would be angry with him. There's no solution I can figure out that will satisfy both of us, and I hate that. I don't want to sneak around or act like I've done something wrong, when I don't think I have. Driving is such a "man" thing! I'm putting Harry's best interests first. (And what choice do I have, really? He's here and he's not going back to the reservation, so the most I can do is keep him safe); I understand he gets angry and doesn't want to be treated like a child, but what other option is left? As Taylor says, "Duh." I don't even think deep down he wants to drive around, especially in a place so different from everything he's known; he just doesn't want to let that pickup go.

Next year Taylor will drive—that's scary enough for me. She really needs us to be focusing on her. I want to make sure she knows that her dad and I are around when she needs us. I figure by doing that, at least we have a chance of catching any potential teenage problems before they start. As it is, I barely have time to check in with her during the day, much less delve into the hidden valleys of high school. This is supposed to be a great time. And another issue—if she discovers I'm lying to Bill, what is that going to model? Is she going to think there are acceptable times to lie to family? The most quality time she and I have had in weeks is spent trying to wrangle her grandfather down to the dinner table—other than that, it's in and out and on with our lives. It's been four months and I'm just so sick and tired of it all. I want my family back.

PSYCHOLOGICAL COMMENT

The never-ending demands of the sandwich generation are familiar. As the character in this story points out, caregiving for the two "slices of bread" is dramatically different. Children are growing towards goals, while elders are letting go and facing losses every day. Many considerations for long term caregiving are expressed by this story, including depression manifested as exhaustion and anger, greater frequency of conflict among family members, and the erosion of the self (the feeling of being trapped or losing identity). It is critical to the ongoing health of individuals and families that these considerations be recognized and addressed before they worsen. Marriages falter and the relationships of parents with children are endangered. Teenage risk-taking may increase because of the combination of need for attention and lack of oversight.

BIBLICAL BACKGROUND

Different from the majority of the Psalms, the "wisdom" psalms are less prayer than proverb. They are chronologically the latest additions to the Psalter. "Happy" or "blessed" is a common translation for a Hebrew expression literally rendered "the happiness of." Psalm 128, like 127 and 144, connects loving children and abundant possessions with a faithful life. The connection appears to go "in both directions"—a person who has such blessings must have been faithful, and a faithful person can expect these rewards. Children are valued both for daily assistance and for the expectation of care for parents in old age. Such a simplistic equation is startling to contemporary ears, at least those of mainline Christians. Certainly caring parents have adult children who seem distant and unfeeling, and toxic parents are blessed with compassionate children. (Similarly financial security doesn't seem a "natural" reward for good living.)

There is some balance in the biblical text itself. Other psalms (such as Psalm 7) are prayers of faithful people suffering terrible experiences, but confident that in the future they will be justified and that the apparent prosperity of the wicked will be transient. (See also Psalm 37.) Jesus' Beatitudes (Matthew 5 and Luke 6) may be interpreted as commentary, balance, or even a contradiction to the philosophy expressed in the wisdom psalms.

QUESTIONS FOR DISCUSSION AND REFLECTION

1. Are "golden years" golden? Have you felt cheated or known someone who felt cheated by the experience of aging or the experience of caring for an elderly person?

2. A common definition of the "sandwich generation" is having an adolescent and an elder in the same household. List some positive and negative possibilities of this situation.

3. Are the gender differences in this story ("driving is a man thing") unique to this family or prevalent throughout our culture?

4. Is lying in family dynamics a strategy you have used or would use? Why or why not?

5. Driving is one of our culture's most potent symbols of independence. Have you had experiences of needing to prevent someone from driving? What was the emotional "fallout"?

ASSIGNMENT: Make a Collage

Take poster board, scissors, glue, and a stack of magazines. Gather every member of your household and read a favorite psalm (such as Psalm 23, 100, or 121). Create an image of the psalm with pictures cut or torn from the magazines. A wonderful way to experience gentle collaboration is to do this exercise in complete silence. Elementary school children will become equal participants when silence is used.

PRAYER

Gracious and loving God, so often it is hard to speak of our real needs, the limits on our ability to give, and our fears of asking for help. Help us to tell the truth—to each other, to ourselves, to you. Help us to trust ourselves that when we feel bad, something is wrong and needs attention. We pray for your grace and trust in your presence. Amen.

9 ⤳ Therefore, a Person Leaves Father and Mother

Genesis 2:24, 26:34–35

No. No way . . . please, I don't think I can stand it. You've done enough. I've put up with enough. If she's here, it's 24/7. No breaks. By default, de-gaying the house. None of our friends will come over. You'll be at her beck and call day and night. I'll be invisible in my own home."

"You're being a little over dramatic, don't you think?"

"Well, if I am it's because we're in over our heads in bad family drama. Theatre Offensive will put us in a one-act contest!" Tom stopped with that one. He knew he was pushing Justin, but he couldn't help it. He was really scared. He hadn't signed up for this when they fell in love six years ago. He knew that Justin and his mother were close and that he went to see her regularly on the weekends, sometimes staying over Monday to take her to doctors' appointments and shopping; but he also knew that Justin had a brother who lived even closer to her, and for some reason hardly did anything.

"Look," said Justin as he stepped closer to Tom, "I understand how you feel. I feel it too, but what am I supposed to do? I was sitting there with Mom and the social worker from the Visiting Nurses Association (VNA). She started talking about how Mom really shouldn't be living alone anymore, how the VNA can't be there all the time, how Mom gets confused and frightened, especially in the late afternoons. She doesn't really need more nursing care right now—she just needs to be around family, not be so alone. She has cancer. I don't have forever with her. I hope I have forever with you."

There was as much challenge as love in the look he gave his partner.
"So let her move in with your brother. You go visit. Every
weekend. Every day! It's OK. I'll come, too. I promise. I'll get to
know her. It will be easier if she's not . . ."

"Underfoot? Was that what you were going to say?"

Tom was quiet. There was no win-win in being defensive.

Justin went on. "Keith's married. He's got kids. He travels. He
won't do it."

Tom felt that something was missing. "Keith's also got a traditional family."

"They aren't close."

Justin's mother didn't approve of his sexual orientation. She ignored it. She never treated Tom like family. Tom's folks joined
PFLAG the week after he came out. They adored Justin. Justin's
mom wouldn't even come to the commitment ceremony—she said
it was "foolish . . . two men can't get married." Still, she was Mom.
They loved each other so much. Justin wondered if she would perhaps have been just as jealous of a woman. She had almost been too
close to her boys. She had raised Justin and Keith without anyone's
help. She had worked overtime to provide them with a good life,
and she deserved to have her sons watching over her now.

Justin had promised to take care of her always, but that was before Tom.

Unfortunately, she and Keith were not at all close anymore. They
used to be; Justin remembered envying the time she spent with his
older brother, but that was before Keith dropped out of college, before he told their mother that he didn't need anyone planning the
rest of his life for him . . . before the baby he'd fathered and aban-
doned. So long ago. Probably he'd been right to do it. Those were
definitely two kids who needed to get an abortion, but his mother
hadn't seen it that way. She didn't care that his girlfriend had been on
so many drugs, the child was lucky to have all his fingers and toes.
She didn't even look at the bruises that girl had given him. Didn't acknowledge that it wasn't always the man who was the abuser.

Keith had picked the one thing that would trump same gender
love.

When Mom and Keith spoke, Justin—in the middle—felt like

he was at risk for frostbite. The worst part of it was, secretly, he was glad to be the favorite. Fifteen years later Keith had the postcard perfect family, but it didn't make any difference. The damage was done. When Justin came out, he worried about how it would affect his relationship with his mother. She was a bit judgmental, he had to admit. Initially, she was fine. In fact, his orientation just didn't exist for her.

It was only after she realized that he and Tom were serious, that this wasn't just a passing phase, that she became upset. Well, not upset. There was just a gap in her attention when the issue came up. Justin was happy basking in the glow of their mother/son relationship, and he couldn't imagine he would have to sacrifice his life with Tom to keep it. It seemed as though both of them wanted him to choose, to play the "whom do you *really* love more" game. He wasn't interested. Justin wanted both. He wanted to be with Tom, to have a family of his own, to stand by this person he had chosen to spend his life with . . . but he also needed to care for his mother.

It didn't seem possible that either of them could ask that of him. Who would ever ask someone they really loved to choose?

PSYCHOLOGICAL COMMENT

A family's ability to cope with difference often depends upon each individual member of the family. Each needs insight, emotional security, and ability to change and grow. These are skills that are usually learned within the family. Sometimes family members choose to minimize or ignore someone's sexual orientation or gender identity because they do not have the emotional tools to deal with conflict. This may work for a while, but it does not support healthy conflict resolution. If a family has engaged in this pattern, then when someone loses independence and needs caregiving, these issues reemerge. In this story, the adult child's desire for approval also reemerges with his mother's need, causing even more conflict in his primary couple relationship.

Visibility is a key issue for same-sex couples. There has been much research to confirm that being "out" is far healthier for a gay/lesbian couple than remaining closeted. Thus, there is much intersecting conflict in this particular story, with no resolution that does not involve loss.

The fact that four of the five stories in this chapter about caregiving in the caregiver's home raise issues of partner/spouse conflict is not coincidental. It is a remarkably frequent result of this eldercare choice with caregivers who have partners.

BIBLICAL BACKGROUND

The two different creation stories in Genesis offer different insights into human behavior and different frameworks for the relationship between God and human beings. The second, "Adam and Eve in Eden," is older than Genesis 1, the poetic six days plus one. The garden narrative concludes with the thought that a person leaves parents and clings to husband, wife, spouse, partner, although the story itself has not yet posited children or, therefore, parenting. This clinging to a primary relationship is cited in the New Testament in the context of divorce (Matt. 19:5, Mark 10:7–8) and sexual and marital fidelity (1 Cor. 6:16, Eph. 5:31). Leaving parents for the sake of discipleship is encouraged in Luke 9:57f and Matthew 8:18f.

The other side of this dilemma—and the other strand in Tom and Justin's story—is pre-figured by the brief story in Genesis 26. Esau's' choice of Judith and Basemath as wives made life bitter for his parents, Isaac and Rebekah. Rebekah even remarked that she was weary of life because of her daughters-in-law (Gen. 27:46). Esau (clueless even for the Bronze Age) tried to remedy the situation by marrying a third wife, Mahalath, Ishmael's daughter, Abraham's granddaughter. (Gen. 28:6–9). The text is unclear whether his parents didn't like the first two wives because of personal characteristics or simply because they were foreigners. Elsewhere there is great fear of the corrupting influences of Canaanite culture. Chances are good that, as in the modern counterpart, lack of experience with a group that is identified as somehow "different" becomes confused when a member of that group is loved by one's adult child. The person who is bothered by the "bitter taste" can't gain enough perspective on the situation.

QUESTIONS FOR DISCUSSION AND REFLECTION

1. Who would be your most challenging in-law? Would religion, race, gender identity, sexual orientation, or language im-

pact that as well as personality? (Don't be afraid to be honest.)

2. It is a factual statement that people leave parents to enter into a marital relationship. Do you think this biblical verse also implies that there is a hierarchy to commitments?

3. What are healthy boundaries that same-sex couples need to set with the family of origin in order to support their commitment to each other?

4. Can you think of ways that Justin, his partner, his brother, and his mother might have addressed these concerns before this crisis emerged? What are some next steps they could take?

5. Are there conflicts and/or differences in your family that should be addressed proactively in order to prevent a crisis?

ASSIGNMENT: Go on a Date

Probably in your caregiving situation there is someone who is making sacrifices because of his or her connection to you rather than to the person receiving care. This may be a spouse, partner, or child. He or she may be a willing participant in the caregiving, a major player, or a reluctant casualty. It doesn't matter. Treat this person to a fantastic evening or day (depending on the age). Go out to dinner or a concert or the circus . . . and don't forget the flowers. Give this person a memorable experience. Surprise! You'll discover you've been on a date yourself.

PRAYER

God, keep rooted the commitments of couples when the responsibilities of elder care threaten to erode the solid ground beneath their feet. We pray especially for those in same gender relationships who are asked to forgive intolerance of the past or ignore new homophobia that springs weedlike from the dust bowl of dementia. In humorless homes, bring laughter; in drab days, bring dates; in the aftermath of angry words, bring the gentle blessing of tears and kisses. Amen.

part three

CAREGIVING WITH THE HELP OF OTHERS

For it is God who is at work in you . . .

PHILIPPIANS 2:13

10 ➥ Sitting on Our Parents' Gods

Genesis 31:19–21, 33–35

Dad decided to move into a new house. It's smaller than the old one, but it's still going to be a struggle. We haven't found a buyer for the old house yet, probably because the neighborhood is "changin"—lots of Southeast Asians. That's why he wanted to go . . . my guess. Anyway he's moving into a black middle-class neighborhood forty minutes away from us. With all the nice little places for sale around here, why couldn't he get close? Stubborn old fool! I've spent hours at the bank going over the paperwork for a mortgage. My father's loans have been rejected in the past, but just let them try to turn him down now! I'll see them in court!

The new place is nice. There are no stairs, not even at the front door, wide doorways for the wheelchair that's coming, and the tub has a safety railing. Even so, he has too many mobility problems to stay alone during the day, and that's the real problem. We hired a caregiver Dad loves, but Jim hasn't been receiving paychecks for a month from his agency, so it's only a matter of time before we'll have to switch to a different one and begin interviewing candidates again.

My father is picky when it comes to companions. And geriatric daycare? Not a chance! Picky is the polite word for it. He doesn't like being cared for by a woman—says it reminds him too much of Mama. She passed two years ago, but he still can't bear to hear her name. He's also been regressing into stereotypes of his childhood; he won't even consider personal services from a Latino or an Asian man. Or a "honky." Oh, boy. That's embarrassing, since it means we have to inquire about race before a candidate comes to the house, and I know the law on that!

My husband washed his hands of it, but I have to respect my father's wishes. He's a product of his time, a proud black man, a man who felt a fire hose more than once. And I'd love him for it, if it wasn't so inconvenient. Who am I to say who can change his Depends? Gerald says I shouldn't make excuses for bigotry of any kind. I know he's right. How can I teach my children that they must extend love and friendship to anybody, regardless of color, when their grandpa spews such hatred? I don't want to expose potential caregivers to his slurs; it's easier to just make his request known.

Jim was a godsend in that respect. He married a white woman, and after the initial explosion, Dad's OK with it. It wasn't much worse than when I first relaxed my hair! Jim brings over his baby girls, and Dad just coos. "Latte" doesn't matter so much when it comes to children. Jim's been so good for Dad. He always knows just what he needs. I hope that when he gets out of his contract with this firm, we'll be able to hire him independently. I know someone in contract law. He's worth it. In the mean time . . .

Sometimes it feels like I spend all my time worrying about who's with Dad, or how he'll pay, or what will happen if his health takes another turn for the worst. He doesn't say anything but this isn't the way things were when he was young—old folks lived with a son or a daughter. He's pushed me at law school with that fire in his eyes and the money he made on the side from the funeral home. He can't take it back now, and I know how proud he is of me and Gerald and what we've made of ourselves, but sometimes his eyes haunt me after I've shut the door. I don't even remember the last time we just sat together and had a nice talk. I used to have the patience to take him out for lunch or to do a little shopping, but now that I'm a partner, I'm busy, and taking care of his business takes too much time. Some days he's just another case to be handled; he's just another nonbillable hour.

PSYCHOLOGICAL COMMENT

Cultural dynamics play a significant role in caring for infirm parents. Generational differences become manifest as family members are forced to negotiate responsibilities. Historically, many communities of color have operated with the assumption that the elderly

would be cared for by family at home. It may have rarely been discussed, a silent assumption. Yet, when adult children pursue career and family choices that require geographical distancing or significant time commitments, these generational and cultural expectations clash.

Simultaneously, as people age, they fall back on what feels familiar and safe. Thus, experiences of ethnically diverse employed personal caregivers can feel overly challenging to chronically or acutely ill older adults, especially if any form of dementia is involved. Sometimes these choices are motivated by principles no longer shared by the younger generation who may treat the concern as merely irritating and—that most feared demon of modern life—time-consuming!

BIBLICAL BACKGROUND

Jacob, with his two wives Leah and Rachel, eleven sons, and one daughter decided to flee his father-in-law Laban's encampment. Jacob complained that he had worked fourteen years for his wives and six years for his flocks, and that his wages had been changed ten times. God encouraged Jacob. His wives, probably still Laban's legal property, were enthusiastic. Rachel went farther than enthusiasm! She stole Laban's household gods, symbols of protection and probably of family authority. On the third day, Laban realized they were missing and chased and challenged Jacob, demanding their return. Rachel had not shared her plan with Jacob, who said he would kill whoever was found with them. He let Laban search the camp, but Rachel hid them in a camel bag and sat on it, claiming she had her menstrual period.

Laban and Jacob made a nonaggression treaty, piling a cairn of stones and eating a covenant meal to seal it. Their prayer, "The LORD watch between you and me while we are absent one from another," testified to their profound distrust of one another and invoked God's watchfulness (Gen. 31: 51–34). The larger story probably reflects an historical boundary pact between Arameans and Israelites over much-contested Transjordan land. In the little story of sitting on her father's gods, Rachel typifies the perennial problem of the changing of values and priorities across the generations.

QUESTIONS FOR DISCUSSION AND REFLECTION

1. Identify something that means more to your parents or their generation than to you. This isn't an issue of disagreement so much as diminished value. Church-going? Volunteer work? Traditional holidays? Voting? How does this affect your relationship?
2. Do people have a right to their prejudices?
3. Business irritations such as a failing home health care agency or mortgage problems often clog relationship time. What are some solutions to "trivia management" that have worked for you?
4. Are there ways that the protagonist in this story can understand and accept her father's limitations without sacrificing her own beliefs?
5. How do we remain the daughters and sons of our fathers and mothers when they need us to be so much more?

ASSIGNMENT: Take a Look at Your Prejudices

List in a "free association" method the types of people about whom you have prejudices. These may be preconceived positive as well as negative judgments. Categories may include race, ethnicity, sexual orientation, economic or educational status, and political or religious views. Write each one on a strip of masking tape or a Band-Aid and tape them on a hand or wall mirror. Look at your face through your prejudices.

PRAYER

O God, you have created us to celebrate our many different colors, cultures, and ways of being. The diversity of life is a gift, and yet, because of illness and fear we turn our backs and hunker down into what feels familiar and safe. Forgive us our limitations and our judgments. Help us to understand and comfort the anxious outbursts of those whom we love, but help us to remain true to what we know is right. Amen.

11 ⇲ Before the Silver Cord Is Snapped

Ecclesiastes 12:1–8

A teenager and his mother are in the kitchen. She has her coat on, ready to walk out the door.

JAMES: I don't want to go.

MOTHER: James, I love you to death, but I'm not going to argue about this. You're going.

JAMES: What's the point? He doesn't even know who you are.

MOTHER: He needs us. He loves to see you, you know. It makes his day.

JAMES: If you're trying to guilt trip me into coming, it's not working.

MOTHER: I don't need to guilt trip you. I say you're going, so you're going.

JAMES: What are you going to do? Drag me?

MOTHER: Don't start with me. He has a doctor's appointment at 4:30, and I want you to sit with him while I pick up his prescriptions.

JAMES : You're not even going to be there? That's not fair. Why do I have to stay if you don't even want to?

MOTHER: I have had it up to here.

JAMES : But it's not fair. You don't even want to see him! He won't remember we've been there five minutes later.

MOTHER: You know what, that's not the point. He's my father, and he deserves to spend time with his family. I know you don't like it there.

JAMES: It smells like a . . . a really dirty men's bathroom.

MOTHER: James!

JAMES: I can't even breathe the whole time we're there. And the nurses are jerks.

MOTHER: What do you mean?

JAMES: They're always yelling at him and they never give him a bath or anything. He just looks so . . . bad. I thought you were going to start shaving him at least.

MOTHER: I do. I just don't have time every week—there's so much he needs.

JAMES: It just seems pointless. Don't you think it would be better if he just . . . you know . . . "passed on?" If someone put him out of his misery?

MOTHER: God help you when you're his age. Just wait until you've lived your whole life trying to provide for your family, trying to be a kind, generous, helpful man. . . . He deserves to be cared for now. He's always been there when I needed him, and now he needs me. Even if he doesn't remember me . . . even if he's never going to be able to thank me or even see me clearly again, it still matters that we go. He taught you how to write your name, you know.

JAMES: Yeah.

MOTHER: He used to take care of you whenever I had to work late.

JAMES: We always got ice cream right before you picked me up.

MOTHER: That's why you were never hungry for dinner?

JAMES: He made me swear not to tell you. He said you would say that he was causing trouble.

MOTHER: He was.

JAMES: I know.

MOTHER: You loved it.

JAMES: He doesn't even get out of bed anymore. He doesn't even watch TV.

MOTHER: There's more to life than TV, you know.

JAMES: I know.

PSYCHOLOGICAL COMMENT

As people live longer, intergenenerational relationships between family members become more intimate and complex. Grandchildren and grandparents know each other better, have more shared memories, and have very different relationships with each other than with the parent/child they share in common. Dealing with the cognitive and physical losses of aging is dramatically counterintuitive to the expansive visioning of adolescence and young adulthood. Developmentally, the youngest generation in a family system is naturally narcissistic (self-absorbed, self-focused, and sometimes selfish). This is a necessary ingredient to the energetic creation of a life well lived. However, it clashes painfully with the need to be present and care for our elders on a day-to-day basis. Thus, it's an issue for every family to manage these opposing forces in a way that supports a creative dynamic across the lifespan rather than a conflict that isolates its members. It isn't easy!

BIBLICAL BACKGROUND

Written around 300 B.C.E., after most of Hebrew Scripture was established (and long after the lifetime of the historical Solomon), Ecclesiastes is attributed to Qoheleth, "leader of an assembly." Because of what is perceived as a cynical tone, there have been several attempts to remove it from the canon. Qoheleth suggested that much of life is "vanity of vanities" or "vapor of vapors." These verses in chapter 12, a famous description of the approach of old age and death, are Qoheleth's final words before a conclusion by the book's editor. The text has occasionally been interpreted as an allegory. "Strong men" can symbolize human legs; "guards," the arms; "women who grind," teeth, "windows," eyes; "almond blossoms," white hair; the gait of the "grasshopper," crutches; the "snapped cord, broken bowl, and pitcher," death itself. Whether these details of metaphor were intended or not, it is a powerful portrayal of the extreme disintegration of a human body.

QUESTIONS FOR DISCUSSION AND REFLECTION

1. Is old age defined by losses or are there gains as well?

2. Is there value to visiting someone who can't remember? Is there training for visiting someone who can't remember?

3. How would you feel if you were someone's "duty?"

4. Should parents force teenagers to visit their older relatives against their will? Why or why not?

5. How can the youngest and eldest in a family support one another's different needs while still holding onto family bonds?

ASSIGNMENT: Write a Dialog with God

One way to do this exercise is to use your dominant hand to write a sentence to God and then write the answer God forms in your mind with your weaker and slower hand. Another way is to fold a piece of paper lengthwise, writing a personal line on one side then turning it over for a response. Only when you are finished should you unfold the paper—the full dialogue will be exposed.

Even if this exercise seems a little silly, try it. Many people have found profound insights with this simple tool. Perhaps the key is that you are writing one thought at a time and then listening for a response from God, rather than sending God a prayer monologue and then returning to (your own) business!

PRAYER

Holy God of all ages, generations, and individuals, you have created us with the energy to dream of our life ahead and the wisdom to appreciate each moment as it comes. Enable us to honor our differences and cherish our connections, to treasure the exuberance of youth and the stillness of age. Teach us compassion as we try to care for those who have cared for us, and help our young to grieve, when grieving is just too hard. Amen.

12   ≈   Golddigger!

1 Kings 1:1–4, 2:4–25

All I'm saying is, he spends more time with Rita's family than he does with us!" Joel leaned back in his seat and stared at the landscape far beneath him.

His brother Louis looked up from the in-flight magazine. "Well, she spends more time with him than we do."

"That doesn't make her family," Joel said. He stared at Louis, but he'd gone back to his reading. "Doesn't it bother you at all? Did he ask about Megan or Cecilia once while you were talking to him? I mean, he has a new granddaughter and he barely glanced at the pictures!"

Louis folded the magazine and pushed it back down into the seat pocket in front of him. He stared over his brother and out the window. "I did think he'd be more excited. I hated to leave them to come on this trip. You know, Cecy never sleeps through the night, and Megan's exhausted by the end of the day." He didn't want to admit how disappointed he'd been with his father this past week. It stung to see how Dad brushed off exciting news in his own family. Louis couldn't entirely blame him though—years ago, he and his brother had not so much left the nest as jumped out of it waving their arms and screaming. They certainly would never have been called close by anyone who had ever met them.

"Thanks for not bailing on me," Joel said. "I don't think I could have talked to Dad alone."

"Do you think we're doing the right thing, putting him in a home?" Louis asked.

"It's not a home. It's an assisted living facility, and you saw the place. *I'd* live there. It has a pool and movies screening every night—somebody to cook every meal—it's going to be great." Joel wasn't kidding; if the place didn't reek of old people, they'd both pack their bags and move in tomorrow. Joel couldn't understand what the fuss was about. This wasn't a nursing home—there was more to do in a day than his father usually got to do all week.

Louis sighed. "But he loves Rita."

"Rita's too expensive," Joel said. "Anyway, I'm sure that after Dad adjusts, he'll forget all about Rita." Yeah right. The way he'd forgotten about how Louis had spilled grape juice on the white carpet in third grade, or how Joel had been suspended for a day back in middle school for letting a little garter snake lose in the science lab. Their father was an elephant—every mistake they'd ever made was imprinted deep in his brain.

"I can't believe we're jealous of his cleaning lady."

"Louis . . ."

"I know, I know, she's his live-in professional caregiver blah blah blah. It doesn't change anything," he said. "It bugs you that he knows all her kids and what they're doing in school . . . we talked more about her family than about the move."

"That's right," Joel said. "I didn't fly half way across the country to get the blow-by-blow of her son's hockey game."

"The house did look good though."

"Yeah."

Louis stretched out his legs as far as he could. "And Dad seemed happy. He wasn't complaining, at least."

"Better than I've seen him in years."

"Are you sure we're doing the right thing here?" Louis asked. "I know we have this planned out, and it does make sense for his long-term care, but I feel bad. If we lived closer, he'd know Cecy just as well. It's not his fault he can't fly out to see us."

Joel turned to stare at his brother. "Are you seriously having second thoughts? We're about to put a deposit down, and I thought we decided that this was best."

"You really don't feel even a little guilty about this? Maybe we could wait a few more months, see what happens."

"Louis, the spot is open now. If we don't take it, we'll have to get back on the waiting list for who knows how long! Do you really want to risk it?" Joel leaned forward to meet his eyes. "We've been lucky that Dad's health has hit a plateau right now, but what if something happens? Is Rita going to be on call twenty-four hours a day? And even if she is, how much is that going to cost us? We have to do this."

Louis closed his eyes. "I just don't want to rush into anything."

PSYCHOLOGICAL COMMENT

Transitions are hard on most families; however, when they involve family members changing roles cross-generationally, they can be even more difficult. Depending on family history, adult children negotiating with and on behalf of their declining parents can raise feelings of anxiety, fear, and anger. Often, understanding how a family has handled transitions in the past will help predict how they may handle this present transition. Resentment of new friends and even jealousy of the close relationships elders have with caregivers is common. It can resurrect long-buried feelings of inadequacy. These brothers may be forcing a premature transition out of their anxiety in their role as "parent" combined with jealousy they may feel in their role as children. Perhaps they and their father should consider working with a professional care-planner or family therapist to navigate this transition more effectively.

BIBLICAL BACKGROUND

David was one of the few kings of Israel or Judah to die in old age. The early chapters of 1Kings show his frailty, his need for a personal attendant—young Abishag the Shunammite—and the conniving of his family and court to take decision making away from him. In fact, after his death, his son Adonijah asked to marry Abishag. This potential alliance with the woman who cared for David during the last days of his life was seen as a power-play by other family members. Abishag only appears biblically as a caregiver and a source of contention. Her own personality—her hopes, her doubts, her feeling toward the old king—were never explored.

QUESTIONS FOR DISCUSSION AND REFLECTION

1. The relationship of an older person to a caregiver can become very close. Sometimes it seems to exclude relatives

geographically distant. Reflect on relief, loss, guilt, or jealousy as emotional responses to this situation.

2. Louis and Joel's father looks "happier than he's been in a year." Have you ever felt you needed to change a relative's situation in spite of their happiness? How did that make you feel?

3. Can good decisions come from suspect motives? How about poor decisions from selfless motives?

4. How does your family handle transitions? In the past have they been welcomed or resisted? Did transitions become crises?

ASSIGNMENT: Make a List of Beauty

Birders keep a life-list of birds they have seen. This week (and this week only, or it could become a chore) write down a list of beautiful things you experience. You can include birds, flowers, sunsets, faces, hands, Christmas decorations, pastry shop windows, natural or human-made music, the scent of hot cider, or the feel of pine needles or ocean spray. Let each of your senses be represented on your list.

PRAYER

Ever-changing and challenging God, we move through so many difficult and important times together as families. Sometimes we feel like frightened children, afraid to venture forth. Other times, we are tired and ache with the weariness of age. May the love that has carried us through the many transitions of our lives empower us to make good choices, grounded in faith that your presence is around and ahead of us. May we guard our childlike hearts from childish emotions, and love as "we have first been loved." Amen.

13 ⌒ Who Are You, My Son?

Genesis 27, especially 18–29

One week several years ago Joanne was a Nielson family . . . of one. The famous TV rating survey couldn't download data automatically in her community, so she kept a written journal. Joanne logged the Weather Channel twice. She was a little smug. She had her job, voter registration, the church stewardship drive, soup suppers at the shelter, tai chi class. Poor me . . . so busy, no time to put my feet up and watch a show. She e-mailed her sister Jane in Hawaii, who was undoubtedly watching Saturday morning cartoons to make sure they didn't have too much violence.

This week Joanne watched television in three doctor's offices. There was a morning show in the hospital lobby while she waited for her aunt's electroconvulsive treatment (ECT), then the country and western channel during Mae's slow recovery. During two football games in her dad's room on the Unit, she answered his questions again and again—who were the teams? what was the score?

Yesterday, Thursday, she watched a PBS special on Alzheimer's at her mom's house so her mother could understand her husband's disease. Joanne organized things so the show followed lawn mowing, the weekly grocery run, and dinner out for them.

"What time do you suppose this show is airing in Hawaii?" Lib Swenson asked her younger daughter. She always asked about Jane. Had Joanne had any postcards? (No.) Did Joanne think Jane would come home for Thanksgiving or Christmas? (No clue.) Couldn't Jane bake just anything—anise cookies, pumpkin pie, brandied fruitcake, cinnamon raisin bread? (Yes.)

When Joanne finally got home after the twenty-four-hour pharmacy drive-through and listened to the message from the facility about increasing Jack's Seroquel, which made that last errand pointless, she ignored the stack of interesting books by her bed, channel surfed for twenty minutes, and fell asleep.

Joanne had quit her job to be available to three elders. She had thought she could keep her activities, but everything became "irregular" in her life and she gave up. They didn't even live with her. Jack Swenson and Mae DeAngelo (who wasn't really Joanne's aunt, but Jack's first wife, Sarah's aunt) lived in a facility, which charged significantly for their care, so what Joanne did all day was a mystery. Joanne's mother, on the other hand, was at home. Lib Swenson's greatest joy was hearing, "Still living in that big house? You're amazing. How do you do it?"

But today was a Friday in apple season and Joanne was turning off her responsibilities . . . and the box. Her pastor had been desperate for chaperones for the youth group apple-picking-and-pie-baking-for-the-fair sleepover. When Joanne volunteered, he was stunned—she'd never had children, much less teenagers. "This is the deal," she announced. "I do the orchard and the kitchen and my "buddy-bunch" delivers a pie to my mom."

The four ninth-grade girls were fine with that. Joanne's mother greeted them politely and immediately forgot their names, but when she leaned over the pie to kiss Joanne on the cheek, she said, gently smiling, "You smell like my daughter." Joanne's heart squeezed. It was ambiguous, but she didn't care.

At eleven o'clock that night her four girls collapsed on their sleeping bags in the church nursery in front of a TV set. "We're going to watch videos all night."

"No way!" said Joanne. "Have you ever gone on a darkness hike—no flashlights? You get used to the lack of light and you can see your way."

"In our pajamas?"

"Why not?"

About ten minutes from any streetlight, they began to see everything clearly. They crested a hill with a strange flat rock—Joanne's goal. The stone was warmer than the chilly September air.

They sat down and looked all around. So quiet. Then the ragged cloud pulled away from the moon.

One of the girls, Haley, said, "Look at the moonlight—it's like a ladder."

PSYCHOLOGICAL COMMENT

Joanne is an example of the "daughter track," a woman who leaves her career in order to care for aging and dependent parents. Women on the "daughter track" (and men who make similar choices) often have to negotiate multiple demands without much recognition by others. Sometimes they become isolated from and resentful towards friends and siblings whose worlds are completely different from their own. Parents sometimes seem to take these daughters (and sons) for granted, while actively seeking connection with those less attentive.

BIBLICAL BACKGROUND

The name "Jacob" sounds like the Hebrew word for "cheat." Isaac, nearly blind with age, sent his favorite of the twins, Esau, to hunt game and fix a special meal before being blessed as the firstborn. Esau had already foolishly given away his birthright to his younger twin Jacob for a bowl of lentil soup, but that transaction (binding in the terms of the text, which is part history and part family myth) was between the two of them. Rebekah, who had always favored Jacob, planned a deception at this blessing occasion involving a farm-bred meal, Esau's clothes with their familiar scents, and kid skins wrapped around neck and forearms to disguise Jacob as the hairier Esau. The behavior of this committed and loving couple underlines just how ancient problems in family communication are!

The plan worked and Jacob got away with an irrevocable blessing. Esau, bereft of blessing, hated him and plotted his death, so Rebekah warned Jacob and arranged a visit/flight to her brother Laban. Alone on his journey, Jacob slept in the bush with a stone for a pillow and dreamed of a ladder of angels, not unlike the Mesopotamian temple stairways of that era. It reached all the way to heaven, and through the vision God promised that Jacob would be protected until he returned. In the morning Jacob celebrated the presence of God in that place and consecrated it as Bethel ("house of God").

This story was told by Jacob's descendants (who continued to worship at Bethel rather than Jerusalem) to prove their ancestor's cleverness!

QUESTIONS FOR DISCUSSION AND REFLECTION

1. How do you think Joanne feels when her mother focuses on her distant sister Jane? How do you think Esau felt about Jacob? Do you know examples of parental favoritism or sibling rivalry like this one?

2. Where does the time go? How can caring for elders who do not live with a person nevertheless become time-consuming?

3. Is there someone in your family who has given up her/his own goals in order to care for parents or other elders? If so, how does the extended family provide support and how does she or he maintain some sense of personal value?

4. In volunteering for the youth group event do you think Joanne is taking charge of her life or fulfilling one more expectation for someone else?

5. Where do we find "ladders of angels" in the overwhelming burdens of caretaking?

ASSIGNMENT: Paint Your Toenails!

A haircut and style, a massage, a yoga class, or joining Weight Watchers will do. This week, do something that cares for or pampers your physical body. You can deal with your mind some other week. In the midst of caring for the body of one or more other people, celebrate your own.

PRAYER

Holy God, it is so hard to know what is right. How much of ourselves do we give to others, and yet still hang onto the soul you have given each of us? Help us to know you as the light in the dark that leads us out of the ordinary and shines anew on all things. Help us to climb ladders with angels in the most surprising of places and with the most unsuspecting of people. Keep us together in love, when our hearts would separate in fear. Amen.

14 ⁀ Spinning Our Hearts Around

Malachi 4:5–6

I exhale as the plane's wheels touch
the ground. Not my favorite mode of transportation! Who would
have thought—Ms. White Knuckle is now Ms. Frequent Flyer? I
flip open the cell phone to call my partner Hannah—no use asking
for trouble by calling later.

"Hey. I'm at Ground Zero."

"It's not that bad . . ." She uses that human service professional
tone of hers. She doesn't say what we are both thinking. What she
does say is "One day . . ."

". . . at a time." It's our code that I've been able to hold onto my
precious sobriety even when flying . . . even when flying to my parents' house.

"You're still taxiing into the airport?"

"Yep."

She asks, "Bill's picking you up?"

"Yep. Old 'why-can't-a-pretty-girl-like-you-find-a-man' Uncle
Bill."

She laughs. "Just like you were a debutante of twenty, rather
than a hardened Massachusetts married lesbian of forty-five."

"Honey, I was never a debutante."

"Yeah, and you'll never be hard as long as you dish out all that
selfless love to family members who gave you nothing but grief
when you needed support." It was an old complaint.

"They're family. They're all the family I've got . . . besides I'm
'the daughter.'"

"I know, I know, even across the country it's the daughter who flies to the rescue!"

We hang up as I pick up my roller board at the jetway and go to look for Uncle Bill's car. His picking me up is indicative of the changes of this past year. Usually, Dad and my brother would argue (good naturedly, of course) over who got to do the airport run. But not now. My once quarterly trips have become more frequent—every six weeks, then monthly. One time it was three trips in six weeks—Dad was having elective surgery, and I had to take care of both him and Mom.

There are three of us adult children. Paul lives only a mile away, but Don and I live in opposite directions, a thousand miles apart. Mom's dementia has been hard on everyone, but mostly on Dad. He's been her primary caregiver for a couple of years. He organizes her medications, cooks healthier meals, takes her blood sugar every morning, gets her undressed and into bed at night. He's worn out and angry. As the only daughter, I am the traditional respite—the one who can tuck Mom in bed at night, and do the intimate things.

In their need, all the disappointments of the past have vanished. Mom doesn't criticize my "mannish" clothes anymore. Dad doesn't overcompliment me when I let my hair grow longer. Sometimes I wonder if I have bought acceptance at the price of whole chunks of time eaten away from my own family and work.

My brother Paul did his share. Now he is in the hospital with a heart attack at age fifty-three. Unless he gets healthier, he's in trouble. So, he's got to focus on himself. I'm not sure how much time Paul spent with Mom and Dad, but his support has been nearby and crucial.

I can't spend more time than I have already—not right now anyway. I always ask myself the same questions: How much is enough? When is a burden acceptable, and when is it not?

There's Uncle Bill in his Buick. "Hey, Cenia Belle, plane on time for once?"

"I believe in miracles. How are the folks?"

"Same-ole, same-ole. But you know, Cenia, I went to the most amazing thing at church. Our church is discussing . . . I bet you know what ONA is?"

All of a sudden I was sorry I ate the hot dog in Detroit. "Yeah. I do."

"There was this great speaker. A gay minister—doesn't that beat all? And he knew his Bible! You know some folks aren't pleased?"

"I bet they're not."

"But I am! I even got me a rainbow ribbon. One for Dot and your Dad, too."

I do believe in miracles.

PSYCHOLOGICAL COMMENT

When family members get sick, we often find ourselves thrown into contact with people we thought we had left behind years ago. When we brush up against one another, the old memories, patterns, and beliefs come rushing back just as quickly. It is important to be clear with oneself and others about one's integrity as an adult. This shapes the way a person reconnects with immediate and extended family. At the same time, it is important to be open to new possibilities. People change. Sometimes they even change for the better! Whether that happens because of time, frailty, and the need for support or because of an important experience, like Uncle Bill with the church program that somehow made more inroads than knowing his own niece for years, it's important to be flexible enough to accept and even celebrate the changes. Appreciating one another's individuality is just as significant as acknowledging family likeness.

BIBLICAL BACKGROUND

"Malachi" means "my messenger" and much of this prophetic book (dating 500–450 B.C.E.) describes a forerunner expected to prepare the way of the Messiah by encouraging faithfulness to the covenant (see 3:1). New Testament Gospel texts often ascribe this role to John the Baptist (Matt. 11:10 among other texts).

The final verses of Malachi conflate the messenger with Elijah, (899–850 B.C.E), a northern prophet who was notorious for his miracles and his dramatic challenge of authority. Second Kings 2:11 describes Elijah's "departure," witnessed by his disciple Elisha, as not so much dying but rather being taken to heaven in a strong wind or whirlwind. It contributed to a belief that Elijah would return. This legend was also tied to Jesus' cousin John with his wilderness wardrobe and diet and his uncompromising call for repentance.

None of these figures—Elijah, the shadowy Malachi himself, or John the Baptist, although he is tied to this specific verse by Luke 1:17—had a particular historical ministry to children and parents. And yet, the verse, describing reconciliation between the generations as a part of ultimate judgment and promise, stands as the very last words of the Hebrew Bible and, for Christians, a prelude to the Gospels.

QUESTIONS FOR REFLECTION AND DISCUSSION

1. What societal factors separate the generations in our contemporary culture?

2. What do you think the role of religious faith should be in connecting generations? Prophetic? Challenging?

3. How often, in your experience, are caregiving responsibilities based on gender identity? Proximity to parents? Preference of parents? Aptitude? A combination of these?

4. List the extra pressures of long-distance caregiving. What are some practical and some emotional solutions or suggestions for these?

5. Are there some hidden potential joys and or obvious challenges that might emerge if your family reconnected around the shared tasks of caregiving?

ASSIGNMENT: Make Paper Airplanes.

OK, this is silly. Make a list of all the stresses in your life. Now write each one on a sheet of paper and fold it into a paper airplane. Fly them . . . at a wastebasket . . . at your spouse or partner . . . out the window. (Retrieve them later.) Feel them go. Now try to experience that same feeling in prayer. Fly it. Feel it go.

PRAYER

Bless, O God, all who are engaged in long-distance caregiving. May each plane trip reach a cruising altitude of peace, each phone call contain a sound byte of unrushed intimacy, every e-mail and every voice mail forward empathy as well as information. And, God, may all your children who are balancing on a wing and a prayer experience generosity and understanding in their workplaces and their homes. Amen.

part four

CAREGIVING—RESPONDING TO CRISES

"So do not worry about tomorrow, for tomorrow will bring worries of its own."

MATTHEW 6:34a

15 ⌇ Let the Dead Bury the Dead

Luke 9:57–62

I have lived in the United States for fifteen years now. I moved here with my wife and our two small children. I was told we could have a better life here and I was willing to believe it. They could go to the best schools and have every opportunity afforded them. It was hard. I was a doctor in Indonesia, and here, I am still only a nurse. My neighbors are kind, as are the people at our church, but it's hard to know I never fit in fully. My son and daughter do, though, and that is why Ameliya and I came. They have no trace of an accent, although they visit their cousins and speak my native language. They belong both here and there. To me, that will always be what I cherish most about our decision—it was the one that expanded the world for our children, the one that showed us they could rise to the challenge.

When we travel back to Indonesia, we go all over the country visiting Ameliya's family. My children are not snobs—they use the outhouses with their cousins, although they are careful with what they eat and drink—and when we come home, they ask when we will go back. My son photographs everything from our most recent trip; he told me he's making a photo documentary of our family and the reunion. It makes me happy to know that he values his Indonesian roots so highly. He's not one of these stuck-up American young men who hates the idea that they come from anywhere else. He makes his parents so proud. My daughter, she's the same way, although she pushes us away more than he does. I'm a faithful Christian, and sometimes I think I am harder on her; I feel it's for her own good, but I also know that we raised her here to be open-minded and strong, to make her own choices, and she does—even if sometimes I wish she would choose otherwise!

On our trip they asked why we didn't visit any of my family. It's not the first time they've asked me, but I've always been vague. When they ask their mother, she says nothing. I didn't want them to realize how angry I am or teach them to disrespect their ancestors. I could not keep putting it off, though; they are old enough to know. "I have no family," I tell them. "My mother is dead, and my father may as well be."

After I tell them this, I can't stop thinking about how long it has been since I last saw my father's face. It has been thirty years since he left my mother and me. I was old enough to take over his responsibilities, to help my mother and to care for her, but I still missed him. We thought he would come back. We thought this for so many years, and I put off coming here thinking he might still come.

Now, a few months ago, I got a letter. He has found me, and he wants to come visit his "son." He tells me nothing of what he has been doing these years, only that he would like to see me. I have lived so long telling people my father is dead that he has become that way to me. This message is like getting word from beyond the grave. I don't know what he wants with me . . . I know I don't want anything from him. He left and he didn't turn back, not for all these years.

I try to figure out why he found me. What could he possibly want from the son he never knew? Is he sick? Does he need money? A place to stay? What could have driven him to do this so many years after the fact? He's nothing to me. I have no father . . . and yet . . . Can I turn him away, after all those prayers? Not in my culture, not in my Christian faith. He is the prodigal father.

PSYCHOLOGICAL COMMENT

Sometimes, when family members are unable to deal with the emotional pain of conflict and dysfunction, they leave. This cut-off between family members can be geographical, financial, physical, emotional, or any combination of these. Dysfunctional distancing is a more common phenomenon that many of us might think. In this story, the pain of abandonment is very real, even if it occurred several decades earlier. In fact, the son has felt so overwhelmed by his father's abandonment that he told others his father was dead, rather than explain the truth to them. Emotions experienced in this kind of loss are rarely effectively worked through; thus, it may seem as real to someone today as during the original event.

Following the pain of abandonment comes the inevitable question of forgiveness and reconciliation. Forgiveness is an important step in the healing of a relationship; however, reconciliation may not be possible. Christian forgiveness does not mean "everything's OK." Without an acknowledgement of one's own painful mistakes, one cannot assume that he or she will be welcome, despite cultural norms. Even with such an acknowledgement, any new relationship is built around the damage done. In this story there are too many unanswered questions and unresolved conflicts for the son and father to reconcile quickly. Success would take a long and mutual negotiation.

BIBLICAL BACKGROUND

Discipleship to Jesus Christ is a priority underlined threefold in this passage and its parallel in Matthew 8:19–22. A first would-be follower was discouraged by lack of shelter or stability. A second asked to bury his father, although it is unclear whether the father was already dead and waiting to be buried (in first century Judea the common practice was burial within twenty-four hours and there were no funeral services) or whether this is a request to postpone discipleship until the older generation passed. This distinction is very important to a modern understanding, which would distinguish responding to a crisis and "putting one's life on hold" for the needs of a chronically ill elder. The ambiguity cannot be resolved in the biblical text.

The third would-be follower simply asked to say "good-bye" to those at home. This mirrored Elisha's request of Elijah (1 Kings 19:20). The younger man, when called to follow the prophet, asked to be able to tell his family. Given permission, Elisha took the plow with which he was farming, broke it into kindling, cooked his oxen and shared them as a farewell meal. Jesus' denial of the request, similar in tone to his "disowning" of his own family when they came to visit him, would have been a sharp contrast to this familiar story for those who heard him.

QUESTIONS FOR DISCUSSION AND REFLECTION

1. What kinds of situations would make you unwilling to reconnect with a family member?

2. Is it possible to value cultural roots and wish to pass them on to the next generation without valuing personal roots?

3. The biblical passage has been used historically by many high-commitment denominations (some of which have been called sects or cults) to divide young adults from their families. Reflect on this use.

4. Cut-offs between conflicted family members are a common pattern in dysfunctional families. Have you experienced this pattern?

5. Can you think of other ways to manage emotional pain and conflict in this story or one of your own?

ASSIGNMENT: Listen to a New Immigrant

Many earlier immigrants to America were without the means to return home for visits. They were often forced into a "don't look back" posture and sometimes tried to assimilate quickly to cultural expectations in the United States. Others, among them many more recent immigrants, value ethnic traditions, language, and family ties. Have a conversation (or interview) with someone who has immigrated recently to this country. Ask about differences in customs, particularly in regard to the role of elders. Ask as well what the person most misses and least misses about his or her country of origin.

PRAYER

God, for everything there is a season—a time to be reconciled and a time to be safe, a time to treasure tradition and a time to make new paths, a time to communicate and a time to weigh communication carefully. Help all those who must make decisions about family connections to do so with wisdom and balance. God, be a good Parent to us all. Amen.

16 ✩ But Naomi Isn't Even My Mother

Ruth

Buzz can't believe how emotionally complicated his life has become. He's glad that he grew up with sisters. It prepared him for the potential turf wars that might happen between these older women in his life. But sisters get over it . . . or his did, and they knew they were family. That was a given. The only way this situation is about one family is the faith way—the way his grandma used to say, "everyone's ever been at the table belongs at the table." She was very clear that meant hired hands, in-laws, and occasional down-on-their-luck "dust bowl cousins" who weren't related to anyone. Panhandlers. Maybe when times are hard, people are more generous.

Eight years ago, when his first wife Shana was dying from breast cancer, he and his mother-in-law, Sherry, became very close; they sat on either side of her hospice bed, their shared grief forging a bond that little could break.

Time goes on, however, and Buzz is now remarried with a wife and young son. Sherry loves them all, and she has always found a place at their table. Unknown to Buzz's new mother-in-law, Sherry is loved like a grandmother by his son, Tucker.

Sherry called. She is having surgery and needs a place to recuperate for a few weeks afterwards. Buzz thinks it's the least he can do. Sherry would have asked her only child to take her in, but she's dead. In her mind, he's still family. Tucker would love it. And Buzz knows his new wife, Jessica, would be okay with it. "Yeah, it's a little weird, but it's the right thing to do. We sure wouldn't want her to go to some impersonal rehab when we have the space." Buzz figures he made a great choice when he married Jessica—she could make steak for two into stew for six and be sure no one knew she did it . . . kind of like his grandma.

The real concern is his mother, Diana, and his new mother-in-law, Janet. Janet lives nearby and comes over a lot on weekday afternoons to play with her grandson. This gives Jessica a break and her mother a chance to stay connected and "do something useful in retirement," as she says. She and her own daughter are as different as they can be and have had difficulties over the years. Grandparenting has healed a thousand little wounds on both sides. Janet relaxes now when she visits—she doesn't even try to suggest Buzz go after the promotion he doesn't want. Now she understands that he needs time to be a daddy.

The problem is that she's never really liked Sherry. More than once she has said things like, "shouldn't she get on with her life and stop trying to leech off our family?" Jessica says Janet must feel threatened, and, when that happens, she lashes out. Jessica even said (in confidence) that Sherry makes Janet realize that her heart is a little like her dress size—petite.

Buzz's own mother, Diana, also seems to think Sherry and he shouldn't continue to be so close. She calls her an emotional panhandler. Wouldn't she be surprised that her words make Buzz think of her own Mama. Too many mamas in this situation—Buzz feels outnumbered. He doesn't get why, but he does know that bringing Sherry into his home for several weeks will seriously upset the smooth operation they have going. And Buzz does like it smooth. After the death of Shana it took him a long time to recover. Now he wonders if he has the strength to deal with all this family drama.

PSYCHOLOGICAL COMMENT

The definition of family is undergoing radical change in our society. "Family" can mean a same-sex couple, a group of intergenerational friends, a couple who had once been related by legal marriage, as well as many other combinations. At its best, to be family together means to join in giving and receiving care and companionship throughout life's journey. However, different people have different levels of tolerance for this understanding of family. For many members of the older generation, family was clearly defined by marriage and blood, with particular roles for men and women. Some individuals may feel threatened or be anxious about too much openness in the definition of family. In this story, the experience of shared grief creates bonds that surpass defining. Experience, belief, need, and creativity serve to create and support bonds of love for many people. However, they may also constrict our openness to others.

BIBLICAL BACKGROUND

Ruth is one of the few stories to focus, not on the nation of Israel, but on a single family. The date of writing is in question. If it were written before the Exile, its purpose would seem to be to establish David's ancestry and encourage the practice of levirate marriage—marriage of a childless widow to a family member to preserve the name and heritage of a deceased man. If Ruth were written after the Exile, it is more likely that its purpose is more political—to oppose the narrow nationalism and antagonism to intermarriage represented by the books of Nehemiah and Ezra through a portrait of the obvious virtue and faithfulness of the Moabite Ruth. Moabites living east of Israel were considered the descendants of Abraham's nephew Lot but they were disparaged for their idol worship. Written at this time, Ruth would fit in with the theology of Jonah and Second Isaiah.

The care Ruth shows her mother-in-law Naomi in spite of the lack of obligation was remarkable in its own context, as well as in ours. The behavior of her sister-in-law, Orpah, who returned to her own parents' house after the deaths of their husbands, was more common. Ruth's words of allegiance to Naomi's future and her country and faith have often been transferred to wedding ceremonies. Ruth and Naomi schemed together for Ruth's remarriage to give them both economic security. Naomi became the caretaker of Boaz and Ruth's baby Obed (the future grandfather of David) thus reversing the personal bitterness caused by the deaths of her husband and two sons.

QUESTIONS FOR DISCUSSION AND REFLECTION

1. Do you value a deep connection with someone who is related to you only by marriage? If the person "biologically" connected to you were removed by death or divorce, would you give up or sever these ties?

2. Do you ever feel that you are expected to make everyone else happy . . . even when they have contrary desires?

3. Read Ruth 1:16–17. Is there someone in your life to whom you can make this commitment?

4. How do your beliefs, needs, and experience inform your choices about caregiving and the definition of family?

5. Can you name the issues that these characters will have to work through in order to make room for one another in their shared lives?

ASSIGNMENT: Cross the Line

This week do something nice for someone else's parent or someone else's child. Send a card or visit an elderly friend or church member. Make a play date with a neighbor or church member's young child or a niece or nephew, or send a college care package to an older one. Reflect on how you feel about this unexpected and completely-beyond-obligation contact.

PRAYER

God, nurture the relationships we chose as well as those that chose us. Do not let death or divorce sever the caring relationships of the past, nor demands from the past stifle new possibilities of human community. Make us all ballet dancers of the family—on point with understanding, making leaps of compassion. Amen.

17 ⮱ Who Are My Mother and My Brothers?

Mark 3:31–35

The multiple sclerosis began—or began to be noticed—four years ago, with her blurred vision and an annoying habit of dropping her keys. When more symptoms appeared, Joyce knew she had some tough choices to make, but she wasn't a stranger to choices.

Joyce believed that people are the result of their choices. She chose the world of ideas, education, and culture. She could have married . . . twice. Honestly, although she enjoyed companionship, even intimacy, there wasn't a man she had met . . . or a woman either, worth the compromises of living together. She loved her apartment in a converted Victorian—a turret with an elevator! She loved the books, the windows, her classical CD collection, and her cockatiel. Joyce loved serving dinner before concerts and hosting holiday parties, but the guests went home. All her college friends had laughed at the "mommy track," but they took it. Auntie Joyce brought honorary nieces and nephews to museums and spoiled them with extravagant gifts. She adored her friends' children but didn't want any of her own.

Joyce was in line to become the director of the Humanities Council. She had the fundraising, programming, and staff management experience that made her a perfect candidate. Anyone who knew her knew that Joyce "was" Humanities . . . until she started dropping her keys. So after some fits of rage and tears, she scaled back her life. Less stress meant better health. She still dropped keys and got tired and tremulous, but acceptance of the reality of the disease helped her to be grateful and enjoy each day. Her job at the Council became three-quarter time and her salary cut meant they could hire a series of bright young interns. The director's position went to a dynamic administrator from San Francisco. Tad and his partner were regulars at her soirees. Joyce convinced herself that she loved being part of bringing culture and ideas into every library, school, and senior center in the state and she didn't need the top job.

With no family and no brilliant career, Joyce lived a balanced life, managing a tricky disease and an extensive social circle. Prior to her diagnosis of MS, Joyce had dealt with depression. It had come and gone over time, sometimes requiring medication. When she scaled back her work she had waited for the gray gorilla to come and sit on her chest. Somehow she had always been able to get out of bed. But now?

Last week she walked into the house to a ringing phone. It was the hospital. Joyce's mother had fallen on the stairs in her apartment and broken her hip. In a panic Joyce went flying out of the house. It started then, and hasn't stopped. Her mom is in bed, needing a tremendous amount of care. She's moving to rehab soon and will be there for some undetermined length of time. Joyce's mother was divorced years ago and there aren't other children. Joyce's aunt, her mother's widowed sister-in-law, lives on the other side of the country.

The social worker took one look at an unmarried daughter living in a spacious two-bedroom apartment in a Victorian conversion—with an elevator—and smiled like the proverbial cat . . . Joyce felt like the canary. Her own doctor was more sympathetic and mumbled something about geriatric daycare, but his bottom line was, "You need to take care of yourself, but you've got to take care of your mother."

Joyce's friends—the ones with the adorable children—had talked about caring for their mothers, fathers, even grandparents, but she refused to accept even the possibility of that scenario. Denial is no longer possible. Here she is—a single (enlightened) middle-aged (vintage) woman with limited finances (an expensive bird) and a progressive illness. Why does she have to be responsible for anything else?

PSYCHOLOGICAL COMMENT

In our society we talk a lot about self-care, yet we rarely realize that the ability to care for oneself requires an interlocking set of variables. Often, when one variable gives way, they all give. Usually the one that comes crashing down is health. In this case, two independent, single women lost their health at the same time, and there was nothing to hold either of them up.

So often, individuals and families operate on a set of assumptions about life without making contingency plans. MS and depression are both autoimmune system diseases. They often coexist. They can both be progressive and fatal. Yet, they can also both be managed effectively, progressing very slowly or staying in remission. Because of this, denial of the potential devastation is a coping tool for many. However, denial of both the reality and the potential for disease, aging, and death postpones or even impedes a healthy response on the part of families, friends, and individuals. Acceptance of reality and good communication with those around us are the keys to solving problems and facing crises as family and friends.

BIBLICAL BACKGROUND

Many gospel texts seem to discourage biological family connections. In Matthew 10:34–39 Jesus claimed that his mission was a sword, which will divide son from father, daughter from mother, daughter-in-law from mother-in-law. In Mark 10:29–32 he promised those who have left family for his sake that they would receive new relatives in the time to come. In Luke 11:27–28 he contradicted a woman who envied the mother who bore and nurtured him by saying that she was less valued than those who hear and obey God's word.

The background to Mark 3:31–35 is Mark 3:21, in which Jesus' family—mother Mary, brothers James, Simon, Joses, and Judas, and sisters (Mark 6:3) decided that Jesus was crazy and that they should go and get him under control. In these verses (parallels Matt. 12:46–50 and Luke 8:19–21) they arrived to do so. Word was taken to him that they were outside and he ignored the summons, praising as his new family those who were surrounding him. This constellation of texts about family is often difficult for modern members of mainline Christian churches fully to understand.

QUESTIONS FOR DISCUSSION AND REFLECTION

1. The "family values" of the gospels focus on a new family, which is not biologically based. Who would you name in your "nonbiological family?" Are there some people who overlap? Is being a single person family a viable and faithful choice?

2. Do you think Joyce is responsible to care for her mother, even if it changes her whole way of life? Would you respond differently if she did not have MS?

3. Explore myths and facts about depression.

4. Denial is a psychological coping mechanism that functions to keep us from being overloaded with painful emotions, thoughts, and physical sensations. Is there such a thing as healthy denial? What makes denial harmful?

ASSIGNMENT: Roll in Someone Else's Shoes

Take a morning, afternoon, or evening and experience a disability. You may be able to borrow a wheelchair or walker—use and stay with the device. You can put paper over the lenses of glasses (safer than a blindfold). Wear ear plugs, or have a friend wrap your hands in gauze. Youth groups often simulate disabilities in this manner and discuss the experience. Even more difficult is to do this exercise alone, but many people with disabilities live alone. Of course, you are never really alone. At the end of the experience, write a prayer for yourself and others.

PRAYER

For all your children with double jeopardy we pray: God, grant them the persistence to protect their own well-being, the compassion to assist those who are dependent upon them, and the wise advisors to help them know the difference. Amen.

part five

CAREGIVING THROUGH ISSUES OF DEATH

"Do not let your hearts be troubled . . ."

JOHN 14:1

18 ⮑ Draw Your Sword and Thrust

1 Samuel 31:1–5, 2 Samuel 1:5–10, 14–16

She had nothing to gain, Natalie Kingston thought. Gina Tursi had nothing to gain from their father's death. In fact, Gina would lose her private nurse job. Natalie was sure, even so, that she'd done it. Gina had killed the old judge. And Natalie was going to make sure she lost her license and went to jail for it—for a long, long time.

The rest of the family had a lot to gain, including Hugh Kingston himself. Natalie and her two brothers alternated days off from their jobs to be with him. Gina and Ann Reilly, the other nurse who came on weekend nights, arrived early enough so they could get home for a late supper, but still—two to three days a week had become a burden. Hugh wasn't getting any better, but he wasn't actively dying. His spirit was. A year ago he still read legal journals, responded with enthusiasm to visits from old colleagues and friends, and had a sneaking fondness for afternoon cartoons. Now when Natalie turned on cartoons, Hugh looked out the window as if she were making fun of him.

The second stroke made him weaker, more despondent, much more sensitive to indignities. He seemed angry at every Depends. When he spilled food off his tray, he'd push it under his bed or wipe it up with the pillow case. "Gina will take care of it," he'd mumble, if she caught him.

"*I'll* take care of it. Spaghetti sauce! I'll put it in to soak. Even then it probably won't come out. Daddy, call me on the monitor!"

Hugh had always favored right-to-die initiatives. He said he would go to a state where physician assisted suicide was legal, when the time came . . . but after the strokes he didn't go anywhere on his own.

About eight weeks ago came a too-casual request that she just leave the bottle of pills by his bed instead of taking them downstairs. Natalie told Hugh she wasn't going to risk her own salvation to cut short God's fullness of time. She warned Bryan and Greg not to give in to subtle or not-so-subtle hints. If their father wanted to go against the commandment, "Do not kill," he should do it alone.

Bryan shrugged but Greg had argued. "How can the old man commit suicide? He can't walk farther than the commode. Hell, he's not strong enough to break a glass and cut his own throat!"

"How dare you talk like that about your own father?"

"I hope when I'm old and sick and no good for anything anymore . . . when I'm a burden on everyone around me . . . that somebody puts a bottle of pills in reach and then goes away long enough that I can sleep my way into the next life."

"Hell. That's what the next life is called."

Bryan broke in. "Hugh's not going to hell just because he can't face another hundred days of laying on his back with his skin breaking down and his mind fogging up. After the *pro bono* work he did . . . the good family man he was . . . and there was never anyone fairer on the bench . . . No one! There's nothing hellworthy in his life."

"Let's help him keep it that way, because I, for one, want to meet him on the other side, and there's a heavenly Judge a lot sterner than he ever was!"

Hugh had become less subtle over the weeks. He'd argued, whined, pleaded. He even tried to get out of bed himself. Natalie planned to buy a locked medicine box.

Hot tears welled up in her eyes. He'd taken a full bottle of Percasset. Bryan and Greg said they were glad for him. She was just a little relieved herself, but what would she say to the minister?

It had to be Gina Tursi. Gina was going to pay!

PSYCHOLOGICAL COMMENT

The right to die with dignity continues to be a controversial and emotionally charged subject. It is important for families to discuss the options and their thoughts, emotions, and theological beliefs as much as possible. For further information, go to www.compassion-andchoices.org, www.endoflifechoices.org, or caregivers support groups on the Internet.

Anger is known to be a stage in the grieving process. Often we misplace our anger onto others when we don't know how to express it, or when we do not know whom we are angry with, or why. Anger is often a defense against feeling the sadness and powerlessness in loss. Perhaps Natalie's anger at Gina and her desire to "make someone pay" is a way to avoid feeling her own loss.

BIBLICAL BACKGROUND

The biblical story is as confusing as real-life. Saul wanted to die before the enemy could capture him and "make sport" of him. At the end of 1 Samuel he asked for help, was refused by his armor-bearer, and, therefore, leaned on the point of his own sword. 2 Samuel picks up with the story of the Amalekite who claimed to have assisted Saul in his suicide, assuming this would please David, whom Saul had repeatedly attempted to kill and who would succeed him as king. Unfortunately for the resident alien, David was not pleased and executed him as a "king-killer." These may be two different accounts of Saul's death rather than a consecutive story. There are three other instances of suicide in the Bible (2 Sam. 17:23, 1 Kings 16:18, Matt. 27:5). In none of these texts is the act itself condemned as sinful, although all have elements of despair. A biblical condemnation of suicide does not exist, but neither can there be found an affirmation of it.

QUESTIONS FOR DISCUSSION AND REFLECTION

1. Imagine how you would feel if someone you love asked for your help to end a difficult and terminal illness. Try imagining some different possibilities and consider whether your response would be different depending on the person.

   If it were my spouse, I would feel . . .

   If it were my parent, I would feel . . .

   If it were my child, I would feel . . .

   (and so on, with other loved ones)

2. Have you ever been close to a situation of suicide? How did you feel?

3. Natalie (and David before her) wants to blame and punish someone. Why is she angry? What would it accomplish?

4. What blessings and dangers would arise from widespread legalized physician assisted suicide?

5. Are you more comfortable with anger or sadness? Can you understand how both are parts of grief?

ASSIGNMENT: Lighten Up

Watch cartoons. Read a children's book. This week lighten your own life as an antidote to the heaviness around you. Norman Cousins' *Anatomy of an Illness* energized a movement to understand laughter as both emotionally and physically therapeutic. Avoid humor that is harsh, vulgar, or based on gender, ethnic, racial, or physical (such as fat jokes) stereotypes. Start to build your own resources of books, DVDs, and comedy clubs that help you laugh. The quickest route may be the youngest. Watch cartoons. Read a children's book.

PRAYER

O God, you have known us since before we were born. Will you know us after we have died? Will you know us if we choose to end our physical life, once our bodies feel ravaged by disease and the effects of modern medicine? Help us to trust you among the complex puzzle of choices. Guide us in our grief so that we may let go of anger and resentment and hold on to your eternal love. Amen.

19 ⌁ Is It Right for You to Be Angry?

Jonah 4

Margaret was evasive when I called. I'd seen her husband Bobby picking out wine at the liquor store for Christmas Eve. I was startled at the change in him. Those bottles would have to go a long way if they were going to gladden anyone's hearts.

"Mags, all I'm saying is, I don't think he's getting any better."

"He's fine," she said.

I tried again. "Didn't you say you had to buy him new pants?"

"Is that some sort of crime?" She asked. "He's lost some weight. He's actually happy about that. He's thinner than he's been since college."

"Isn't that a little unusual for a fifty-five-year-old man?"

"Janet, cut the third degree. I said he's fine, so he's fine."

"Is your mother-in-law still coming tomorrow?" I asked.

Margaret sighed. "Unfortunately. She's staying for a week, did I tell you that?"

"You might have mentioned it."

"I already know what's going to happen," she said. "He's going to make himself sick trying to keep her happy, and when she's gone, he'll be a mess. She sticks it to him—all about how wonderful his father was. I literally had to put my fist into my mouth at Thanksgiving to stop myself from jumping in with, 'Father of the Year award goes to the most dysfunctional man on the planet, Bob Evans.'"

"I thought he used to hit her," I said, thinking back to the year before, when Bob Sr. had passed. Before the funeral, Margaret had tried to console her husband, who was wracked with guilt that he'd never managed to forgive his father.

"He did!" she replied. "He was a bastard, but to hear her talk, he was an absolute saint. I swear to God, she sets back women's lib fifty years at least."

"Maybe she's in denial," I said.

"I'm sure she is, but . . ." She trailed off. I figured she was probably thinking the same thing I was. You can only go so far attacking a woman who spent her life a victim. "It's just not fair. Bob did so much for his dad those last few years, but when it comes down to it, it doesn't count. He didn't *feel* it. It's made worse by the fact that Bob really tried to 'make it up' in the end. He knew he'd been a bastard and he tried to give big presents and be the 'grandpa family man' that he never was when Bobby and his sisters were growing up. Bobby let him back into our lives but their relationship was too far gone, and now he's the guilty one. One more kick in the head from the champion kicker! If his mother could talk about the reality of the past, maybe he wouldn't. . . . I don't know. I don't know what to do anymore."

"He won't talk about it with you."

"I don't think either of us knows anything new to say."

I didn't know what to tell her either. Margaret needed to admit that Bobby was still having trouble coming to terms with his father's death—and that she, too was involved. She needed to talk about it with someone, to allow herself, for once, to lean on someone else. Maybe me.

"I don't know if I'm going to get through this week," she said.

"Of course you will."

"What am I going to say to her though? She doesn't even know what Bobby's going through. It isn't fair."

"I know," I said, "but what are you going to do? If he doesn't want her to know, do you really want to get in the middle?"

"You're right," she said after a minute's consideration. "She and I can't even agree on what constitutes 'clean.'" I can't imagine what would happen if I tried to tell her that her son was in the middle of a nervous breakdown because she can't talk to him about his childhood."

"Can he at least talk to his sisters about it? They were all there—they must remember what happened."

"They've talked, of course, but Gina's ten years younger than he is, and Alice, twelve. He was responsible for them and tried to keep them out of the house as much as possible when they were kids. I don't think he wants to bring it up with them any more than he has to," she replied.

"So," I said, "the two of you are pretty much on your own."

PSYCHOLOGICAL COMMENTS

Memories from childhood, which may have been long forgotten, often resurface during times of transition, loss, and death. Increased contact with family members, as well as intense emotional moments with siblings and parents, can cause someone to be flooded by memories, images, and feelings. We can feel forced by the finitude of death to "forgive and forget" in order to achieve the resolution for which we have longed. When we can't make it happen, we feel guilty. Forgiveness cannot be forced. Abuse cannot be forgotten. Can individuals and families create new ways of being in relationship, new meaning in their lives together, and new hope for the future? Yes, sometimes.

BIBLICAL BACKGROUND

Jonah was desperately angry because God forgave the Ninevites when they repented. He had to be swallowed by something much bigger than himself to be forced to preach repentance to this enemy people in the first place. In this less well-known story of this little book, God offered the sulky prophet a parable of the shady bush that grows in a day and the worm that consumes it. Jonah developed a fondness for the brief life of this bush and God was able to liken this feeling to God's own love for the wicked but repentant Assyrian people. It was an odd tactic, but God does not seem to be proud when it comes to helping people understand themselves.

The book of Jonah is unique in prophetic literature by being an uncomplimentary mini-biography rather than the recording of a prophet's words. The historic Jonah lived in the mid 700s B.C.E. and is recalled by only a brief biblical note (2 Kings 14:25). These four chapters, with their folk tale flavor, were written by a storyteller of the 500s, who felt that the narrow nationalism of the post-Exilic people, which bordered on "ethnic cleansing," was not a faithful response to God's generosity. The book ends on a question—addressed to Jonah—but certainly intended for hearers and readers of the tale.

QUESTIONS FOR DISCUSSION AND REFLECTION

1. Have you known anyone who "rewrote" history like the mother-in-law in this story . . . or have you done it yourself? Share as much as you are comfortable sharing.

2. Bobby, like Jonah, is being poisoned by anger and guilt that have no outlet. Do you ever feel that your present is controlled by your past? (A particularly sensitive example of this is the situation where someone has died and gone beyond either confrontation or reconciliation.)

3. What are your definitions of forgiveness? Discuss (or even debate) the relationship of forgiveness to an abuse situation. Reflect on the prayer sentence, "Forgive us our sins as we forgive those who sin against us."

4. A spouse is an inside outsider in some families. What practical suggestions would you offer Margaret?

ASSIGNMENT: Don't Fix It

Set aside five half-hour time blocks this week for telephone calls. (Or four or three . . . don't overburden yourself.) Choose five people you know who have significant issues in their lives. Pray for five minutes before you call. Listen for twenty minutes using easy nondirective questions. Just listen. Some of the conversations may be whiney or circular. Just listen. You may be pumped for advice. Just listen. After twenty minutes complete the call so you don't become overwhelmed or even irritated. Finish this gift of time with five more minutes of prayer for the person with whom you were talking.

PRAYER

We sometimes wonder where you are, O God, when families live and die in pain. Protect us from harm—from the danger of hitting or of being hit. Speak to us and through us when it is time to forgive, not too quickly, not too easily, but only honestly with the spirit of grace and power. Enable us to love and forgive ourselves as we have loved and forgiven others. We pray in the Spirit of the One who stood firm in his beliefs, when others would have had him change, in the Spirit of the One who holds us each accountable for love's sake. Amen.

20 ⁀ Blessed Be the Ties That Bind

Genesis 25:7–11

Her mother's dying brought her back to this place. She hadn't been here in two years—had made excuses at Thanksgiving, traveled at Christmas—there was always a reason that bordered on ingratitude. Susanna knew that. She knew her mother was angry at her for it, and that hurt. She wasn't trying to offend her mother. She was trying to avoid her sister. She wouldn't come out and say it, but she was.

Her mother could never understand that. Susanna and Shannon were her precious girls. They were her proof that God still answered prayers, even in this modern day. She had loved them so much more because of it, because they were a special gift—the unexpected miracle. It was really a burden too great for either of them.

They were identical twins—closer than most sisters ever could be. Their mother had given them everything she could think of, and then some. She'd tried to shield them from the bitter divorce, from the custody battles that sent one daughter to live with her father and left one in the house in which they'd grown up.

Susanna had never forgiven her sister for getting to stay.

It wasn't just the cramped apartment and the second-hand furniture, or the separation from her mother and her friends. It was the loneliness. The constant ache of being separated from her sister and, to a lesser degree, her mother, was unbearable. Susanna's father worked two jobs, and she could count the conversations they had when he was home on one hand. She spent long afternoons wandering around the neighborhood, situated at the edge of an industrial park, or watching the little black and white TV in her room.

She missed Shannon more, rather than less, as the months passed by, but there was nothing she could do.

She ate less and less, became a shadow of herself, until even her father noticed. She was in and out of the hospital as they tried to treat her eating disorder, tried to force the life back into her, but nothing helped. Finally, finally, they'd sent her home.

Home to where her heart lay, with her sister and her mother. It should have gotten better, but it didn't. When Susanna arrived, she was gaunt and, in her own eyes, ugly. Shannon, in comparison, was lovely—physically beautiful, an accomplished student, and the apple of her mother's eye.

Shannon and their mother tried. The logical part of Susanna's brain accepted their efforts, but somehow, it was never good enough. It wasn't going to be the same. Instead, resentment replaced longing, until all she felt for her sister was bitterness. It didn't have to be this way, she knew, but that was the path she'd started down, and it was too late to change.

Even here in the hospital, their mother lying between them, Susanna couldn't think of anything to say. This was the life she'd chosen, and sitting together, their strongest tie fading away, the road seemed too long to retrace.

PSYCHOLOGICAL COMMENT

This story painfully reminds us that sickness and death do not occur in isolation. They are deeply connected to the realities of our lives. Dysfunctional family patterns and unresolved conflicts do not magically go away so that we may deal with the dying. In fact, they are sharply brought into focus no matter how long it has been. When we gather around a deathbed, we bring our whole selves to the experience, even if we would rather not. The psychological complexity of children who are multiples calls for particular therapeutic assistance in times of stress.

Eating disorders occur within a family context, raising feelings of pain and fear in all family members. Finding ways to acknowledge the realities we have known together over the years can enable family members to let go of the past and be fully present to the experience at hand.

BIBLICAL BACKGROUND

This biblical passage needs "family history" just like the deathbed scene in our vignette, "Blessed Be the Tie That Binds." Sarah died at one hundred twenty-seven years. Abraham bought the cave of Machpelah in the field of Ephron, son of Zohar the Hittite, who lived east of Mamre. (Gen. 23) The negotiation was complex and public because Abraham insisted on a purchase so that he could own land in Canaan. The four hundred shekels of silver, which Ephron called cheap, was actually an exorbitant price. Eventually, Abraham, Sarah, Isaac, Rebekah, Jacob, and Leah were buried in the cave of Machpelah, which is located traditionally under the Muslim Mosque of Abraham in Hebron.

Much earlier than that, Sarah, jealous of her maid Hagar, and Ishmael, Hagar's child by Abraham, had driven mother and child into the wilderness. Ishmael at the time was a small boy (Gen. 21). Only God's angelic intervention kept him alive. The name Ishmael means, "God hears." During his lifetime, Abraham gave gifts to Ishmael and the children of Keturah, the woman he married after Sarah's death (Gen. 25:1–6), but his entire legacy was reserved for Isaac. Nevertheless, after Abraham's death, Ishmael returned to help his brother Isaac bury their father next to Sarah. It must have been emotionally wrenching.

QUESTIONS FOR DISCUSSION AND REFLECTION

1. What are some of the ways in which sibling relationships are challenged by the circumstances of the death of a parent? Have you experienced similar situations?

2. Are there possibilities for sibling relationships to be mended or improved, which emerge only after the death of a parent?

3. Can you imagine ways that these sisters could be reconnected more effectively? Have you had similar experiences in which you felt a personal relationship slipping away but were unclear how to hold on?

4. How can wakes, funerals, burials—the ritual activities around death—offer a return to holy ground?

5. Are there ways in which eating disorders, addictions, or dysfunctional behaviors have impacted your ability to be present to someone actively dying? (Do you or a family member need help in the present with any of these? If so, please speak to a pastor, counselor, or friend whom you trust.)

ASSIGNMENT: (There is a choice of assignments this week)

Learn about eating disorders: If you don't know much about the deadly eating disorder anorexia, take time to read a couple articles about it and similar diseases such as bulimia. Take your empathy on an excursion from the issues of eldercare. Although these diseases have been highlighted by the media over the last twenty years, they've been around for a much longer time.

Make a family recipe. Choose a recipe that you associate with happy times. It should be something you have not cooked for at least a year or that you have never cooked yourself. Don't worry about seasonal appropriateness. There's something to be said for January s'mores and August gingerbread. Feed your recipe to someone you love.

PRAYER

Holy God, sometimes we carry so much pain. The hurt we harbor constricts us from our real selves and holds us back from those around us. We often need each other to fully release it. Help us not to be afraid to reach out—to really reach out—to one another and to risk forgiving each other and ourselves so that, together, we can embrace a new and daring future. We pray in the Spirit of the Risen Christ, who risked everything and forgave all. Amen.

21 ⌇ Now Let Your Servant Depart in Peace

Luke 2:25

Enuma leaned over and kissed her son. He snuggled down under the covers and smiled sleepily up at her as she reached across him to turn off the lamp. She sat a moment longer in the darkness listening to him breathe before she stirred. Down the hall, she could hear Eli putting Maya back in her crib; she peeked her head in the door, but let them be. He worked such erratic hours, he relished any opportunity to spend time with the kids.

Instead, she let herself out onto the porch. They screened it in during the summer to keep the mosquitoes at bay, and although it was too chilly for insects now, she still enjoyed spending time here. The stars were much clearer in the cold air, and she could pick out a number of the constellations. She was still tracing the curves of Orion's belt when Eli joined her on the swing.

They sat quietly, listening to the sounds of their daughter singing herself to sleep. Eli reached over and massaged Enuma's neck. "Did you get over to see your father today?"

She sighed. "I did, but he wasn't awake. Linda says he's been sleeping most of the day all week. He hasn't been eating either. I sat with him for a while anyway."

"Did the doctor stop by?"

Enuma leaned back and stared out at the sky. "She did."

"And?" he prompted.

"It's not good." She reached over and squeezed his hand. "You know, when I was a little girl, I didn't think my parents would ever die. I don't think anyone does, but I really believed it. Then, when I graduated from college and moved out here, I started thinking that they should never be allowed to die. They should never leave me alone." She glanced at her husband, then wrapped her arms around her chest tightly.

"You aren't alone," he said softly.

"I know. I wasn't alone then either, but still—it was just the feeling that time was moving too quickly, and before I could really get to know them they would be gone."

"You spend plenty of time with your father," he said. "No one could ever say you neglect your duties . . . "

"I know that's true. I'm not worried about what people will say or think. I just feel like I'm being cheated. He's only seventy; he should have ten good years left."

"He's unhappy, though. You know he is. Maybe this is the best thing for him," Eli said. "I can't believe I'm even thinking this, but maybe it's time for us to let him go. It could be that's what he's waiting for."

"So what should I do? Encourage him to die? I can't do that."

"I'm just saying maybe we're being selfish. We had all these plans. James and Maya were going to grow up knowing their grand-parents. We were going to invite your parents to move in when they gave up their house, but since your mother passed, the life's just gone out of Dad. It's like he can't even bear getting up to face the day."

"He'll move on. It just takes time. It's hard for me too—some days I feel like I want to stay in bed. But we can't just give up, " Enuma said, "It's not right. It's a sin to squander the life God gave us. I won't ask my father to do it."

"It's not up to you though," he said. "We can keep going this way, and I will, if that's what you want to do, but ultimately, he's the one who will decide—not us."

She was stubborn. "He'll choose to live. I know he will. The fight hasn't gone out of him yet; he just needs a little more time to see that."

"I just don't want you to get your hopes up . . . I'm afraid of what could happen if you don't allow for the possibility . . ."

"I'm allowing for it. I just don't think God will let it happen. And if I don't have my faith, what do I have?" Enuma replied.

"Nothing," he said softly. "Your faith is something I'll always love about you."

PSYCHOLOGICAL COMMENT

The experience of loss is multilayered within this family. Often, old age is an experience of letting go. There are many potential losses —the loss of physical agility and strength, the loss of work, the loss of a home, the loss of friends, and the loss of a spouse/partner. The process of coming to terms with these losses varies individually depending upon life experience, personality, spirituality, and the support of others. And, yes, some people die in the year after the death of a loved one. It used to be called "dying of a broken heart." It is still a mysterious reality.

The experience of the death of one parent can be filled with sadness; however, the death of the second parent can fill a person often with extreme anxiety, as if the last living parent served as a buffer between the child (no matter how old) and the vastness of the great unknown. In these times, one is faced with one's own mortality and the fleeting nature of life, in addition to the experience of grief.

BIBLICAL BACKGROUND

The words of the elderly Simeon, who lived in the Temple because it had been revealed that he would not die before seeing the Messiah, have liturgical familiarity as the *Nunc Dimittis* in the funeral service—"now let your servant depart in peace." Christian families are encouraged by these words to "let go" of those who have already died. The words are actually taken from the Latin manumission of a slave. In the original story Simeon rejoiced in seeing the child Jesus presented in the Temple with the appropriate sacrifice of turtle doves for Mary's purification after childbirth. Then he blessed the whole family and offered a disturbing prophecy that Jesus would bring about the rising and falling of many and be opposed, and that a sword would pierce his mother's soul. Then the old man's work was finished. Perhaps Simeon had a family for whom that was hard.

QUESTIONS FOR DISCUSSION AND REFLECTION

1. Have you ever wanted someone to live longer because you had plans for them? How did you feel? Do you feel empathy for Enuma's love for her father . . . or is she selfish?

2. Do you think it is ethical to offer "permission" to someone to die?

3. Can grief, like the father's in this story, contribute to death by illness, or to death without an illness?

4. What are some sources of strength and hope that individuals and families need to count on in difficult moments like this?

ASSIGNMENT: Pray for Caregiving Strangers

You are going to see one or more people this week whose story you'll never know. Maybe you'll see her in a doctor's waiting room or hospital lobby. Maybe you'll see him in a pharmacy line or moving furniture into an assisted living facility. Pick this person or family and memorize visual details. Hold them in prayer and do so again every morning and evening for seven days. For example: "God, remember the woman with the Patriot's sweatshirt, blond hair, and tears in her eyes in the ICU waiting room? Give her comfort, strength, and patience and hold in the palm of your love the one for whom she is caring. Amen." Expect your heart to open up as you pray, not just for the issues that are constantly surrounding you, but those of others.

PRAYER

Holy God, you are the creator of all that is infinite and unknown to us. Yet, you also have known each of us "before we were knit in our mother's wombs." When we are afraid, when we are lonely, when we worry for ourselves and others, help us to count on your presence. Help us to trust that, as we have known you present in the many changes of our lives so far, you will be with us through all the transitions to come. May we be mindful that you and your creation are always trustworthy. Amen.

22   ∽   Do You Love Me? Feed My Sheep

John 21:15–19

She had always been a feeder of lambs. Marilyn looked in the mirror. Mary Pipher in *Another Country* called it young-old, the era of energy and curiosity combined with free time and lack of commitment. Young-old was a time to travel, learn new skills, and enjoy friendships before becoming old-old curtailed even ordinary pleasures. Marilyn was there—postmenopausal zest and best health-club-weight-watcher shape of her life. She had lots of friends. She had colleagues who even promised her (at that wildly silly retirement party) that they would call her in as a consultant. She had told them she was taking retirement at sixty-three and announcing it at sixty-two because she wanted to train her replacement. Lauren would be fantastic— she had climbed every rung of the ladder just as Marilyn had at forty-seven, when Keith's coronary set her down in a valley so shadowed she wanted nothing more than to follow him.

Yes, she had thought a lot about suicide then, but that was the summer Kristen was pregnant with her first baby and Beth was planning her beautiful October wedding. After the neighbors left them with a Mt. St. Helens of steaming casseroles, Beth had turned to her, unshed tears glistening in her eyes, and asked, "Mom, will you walk me down the aisle?"

Marilyn turned her face back to life. Even if life insurance was going to pay the mortgage, somebody would have to pay for the wedding. She began with part-time tutoring of third graders at Math for Mindfulness, a sincere, disorganized "collective" that focused on happy, competent children rather than successful grades. Marilyn took over office management, then the expansion to other towns and other subjects, and finally the decision to hire only teacher/mentors who had themselves experienced a learning disability or academic setback and could empathize with their students. Brainbows was born.

Marilyn had been feeding "lambs" intellectual nourishment for fifteen years, and before that she had her own girls. Now she was planning on keeping up with her not-too-lamblike grandchildren who wanted to teach *her* that "manga" was not Italian for "eat some more." She was going to travel—Barcelona, the fjords of Norway, Thailand, Wyoming . . . and just before other people would notice something was wrong, Marilyn was going to fall off one of the Rocky Mountains.

There were things she was already quietly doing—ginkgo, folic acid, blueberries, strawberries and spinach, square-dance and crosswords, a Spanish class for the Barcelona trip. And she was taking Aricept. Not Namenda. Not yet.

Marilyn really retired early so she could enjoy the next five to eight years and then depart before she lost her dignity. She had seen the effects of Alzheimer's and was determined not to be a burden on the kids. They had their own lives to get on with—if she hung around for twenty more years, she would only suffer . . . and they would have to watch her suffer. It was not the way she wanted to be remembered. She never wanted to look out at them from a bed she couldn't leave. Her ancestors—the ancient ones anyway—hadn't gone out that way, and she didn't plan on it either. Maybe she wasn't going to have a big party and then get pushed from a lakeshore on a burning boat, but she didn't have to die lying down!

When her never-married Aunt Elizabeth, sharp as a tack, her favorite aunt and Beth's namesake, got in touch to ask if they could move in together, Marilyn was stopped cold. How could she say no? Elizabeth was eighty-six and promised she would stay out of Marilyn's way—feed the cat, read the mail during Marilyn's trips. They would get a three-bedroom apartment so there was always room for grandkids. Marilyn didn't want to tend any shrewd old sheep. Elizabeth only needed a little bit of extra help to stay independent now, but in five years? In five years Marilyn certainly didn't want to be taking care of Elizabeth and she certainly didn't want Elizabeth to even consider taking care . . . of her.

PSYCHOLOGICAL COMMENT

The cycles of generativity—nurturing, caring, and maintaining—are a major theme for all of us as we understand our relationships with others over time. The key to a life of fulfilling generativity lies in the experience of balance. If we are always nurturing, caring, and maintaining, then we are out of balance. Being out of balance can lead us towards despair and depression, and, in fact, away from others rather than closer to them.

Culturally, we act as if our out-of-balance, overworking lives will be rewarded in retirement. Then we are harshly reminded that we are not in charge—the best laid plans go awry with illness—our own or others.'

Suicidal thoughts can recur in life, and diagnosis of illness is one of the most common causes. In this case, somewhat unique among these stories, the "shrewd-eyed" elder may be offering care to a member of the "caregiving generation."

BIBLICAL BACKGROUND

The third resurrection appearance in John takes place by the Sea of Tiberius (another name for the Sea of Galilee or Gennesaret) where some of the disciples had a bad night fishing. Jesus appeared on the shore, directed their cast, and cooked them a breakfast of charcoal broiled fish. His question to Peter, repeated three times, mirrored Peter's three denials of Jesus. The prediction of Peter being bound and led where he would not wish to go is usually related to the tradition that Peter was crucified upside down by Nero in Rome around the years 64–68. Commentators frequently note the Greek distinctions between words for "love." Jesus used "agape," or self-giving love, and Peter responded with "philia," the love between friends. The shifts between lambs and sheep and tending and feeding may also have significance.

The bottom line of this confrontation between Peter and Jesus may be that Peter thought he knew what following Jesus entailed, and Jesus was warning him that the situation could change but that the love would not.

QUESTIONS FOR DISCUSSION AND REFLECTION

1. What diagnosis would cause you to consider suicide?

2. Marilyn has given to others throughout her life. Should she be allowed to choose her retirement plans and death? Do you think she should discuss it with others?

3. From your experience, what suggestions can you offer for people across the generations to help others find wholeness? Can older persons help younger ones as well as younger helping older?

4. What particular message does the resurrection have for people who are aging?

ASSIGNMENT: Go Deeply into the Bible (Even If You Don't Have a Fishing Net)

Choose a biblical chapter for the week—just one. John 21 is a good choice, or Matthew 5, Romans 12, 1 Corinthians 13, or one of the Psalms. Read your chapter three times a day very slowly. Try reading it indoors and outdoors. Discover whether there is a musical version or a hymn based on it. At least once, read it aloud. Let it give you new insights every time. Make a friend of the text. Journal your discoveries.

PRAYER

O God, you have made us for one another, and you have called us to be faithful to you. May we know the spirit of resurrection throughout the cycles and changes of our lives. Help us to trust one another in the sharing of nurture. Help us to feed one another, without forgetting to eat ourselves. And help us to know you through earthly life, death, and life eternal. In the Spirit of all that is holy, we pray. Amen.

part six

H I D D E N   S T O R I E S

Walk humbly with your God.

MICAH 6:8

23 ⁊ The Children's Children

1 Samuel 3:3–18

Kira, fifteen years old, is on the phone. From the couch, her grandmother calls.

GRAN: Kira, I need you!

Kira (into the phone):"And then I told Josh that I would meet him after lunch, but he never showed up. Serena was with me, and she was so mad. She said . . .

GRAN: Kira!

KIRA: I'm on the phone.

GRAN: It's time for my bath. Kira! Please—

KIRA: I'll be there in a second, I said.

GRAN (after a minute):Kira!

KIRA (into the phone): I'll have to call you back, okay? Oh, yeah? I'll see you at school tomorrow then. Bye. (She stands up and helps her grandmother off the sofa.) I said I'd be right there.

GRAN: I always have my bath at seven o'clock. It's after seven now.

KIRA: I know, but I haven't gotten to talk to Jamie all week. I just thought . . .

GRAN:You just thought you could leave me here.

KIRA: No.

GRAN: I understand.

KIRA:You know that's not it. I don't mind helping you with your bath . . . or making you supper . . . or getting you into bed. I just wanted a chance to talk to my friends.

GRAN: I'm such a burden on this family, aren't I? That's why your father's never home. He can't stand to look at me. I just drain the life and happiness out of you and him.

KIRA: You know that's not true. He's working, Gran. He has to work a lot of hours right now. He can't turn down overtime to be with us. In the winter, he'll work less. There aren't many houses that can be painted when it's so wet outside.

GRAN: He's never here.

KIRA: I know, but I'm here, and I can help you.

GRAN: You're at school all day. It's too quiet here. I have no one to talk to. And when you come home, you're always on the phone.

KIRA: I'm sorry. I know. I should take you out somewhere. Would you like that? We could go out for dinner or something after I get my license.

GRAN: After that, you'll never be home. You'll just drive off every day. Just like your father.

KIRA: I won't do that, I promise. I'll still be here to help.

GRAN: You both would just love to see me shipped off to some home, wouldn't you? Well, I'll have you know that I won't let you. You don't do that to family, and like it or not, we're family.

KIRA: We would never do that to you. We've never even talked about it.

GRAN: You're lying. I know you are.

KIRA: I'm not. I swear.

GRAN: It's just this hip, you know. My mind is still working just fine.

KIRA: I know.

GRAN: I could probably even help you with that schoolwork of yours.

KIRA: Know anything about algebra?

GRAN: It's math, right?

KIRA: Yep.

GRAN: You wouldn't know it by my checkbook, but I used to be a real math whiz.

KIRA: Oh yeah?

GRAN: Let's take a look at it a little later. Maybe we can figure something out.

KIRA: That would be nice, Gran. I'd really like that.

PSYCHOLOGICAL COMMENT

When an elder is cared for at home, all of the family is affected. We often think about adult children as the primary caretakers; however, teens and even children are also involved as secondary or even primary caregivers. Statistics show that an amazingly large number of elders are the responsibility of teenagers after school. Studies are currently tracking the effect of this pattern on the academic achievement of the adolescents involved. Certainly the potential for after-school activities, sports, part-time jobs, and social life is dramatically affected. Most articles about this phenomenon warn about the damaging effects on teenagers when they are given this responsibility.

Our society operates on an assumption that teenagers and elders have less in common than any other pair of age categories and would not be interested in communicating with each other. Sometimes just the opposite is true. Teens and elders can give each other the gift of attention, which both need. Finding ways to relate to one another beyond the necessities of giving physical care is fulfilling for both. Older adults and teenagers have deep longings to be useful and meaningful in the lives of others. Together, they can become both. However, although it is important to involve teenagers and children in the care of elders, it is also important to remember that they are not just little adults. They are primarily focused on their own development and self-differentiation from the family, and they need guidance and relief in their role in family caregiving.

BIBLICAL BACKGROUND

First Samuel may have developed from three sources, but it is now a single coherent account of Israel's problematic transition to a monarchy. Hannah's story (chapters 1–2) takes the classic form of an older barren woman receiving an unusual child as God's gift.

Having prayed for a baby, she promised to consecrate him at three years to be raised in the temple at Shiloh. When he was born, she sang a psalm of personal joy and thanks for justice, which became the model for Mary's Magnificat (Luke 1:46–55). The conclusion of chapter 2 is a condemnation of the high priest Eli's two sons Hophni and Phineas for immorality and extortion.

Blind, and neglected by these sons, Eli is cared for by Samuel, who was the age of an adopted grandchild. In chapter 3, Samuel had gone to bed in the temple after tending the old man and the lamp of God. God called him. Three times Samuel went to Eli expecting one of the priest's querulous needs. Eli recognized God's call and told Samuel how to respond to his first vision. In the morning, Eli asked Samuel for the truth contained in that vision, even though he realized it would be bad news for his family. Across the absent generation, Eli and Samuel communicated their care for one another and their integrity before God on the eve of national chaos. It is a brief and beautiful picture.

QUESTIONS FOR DISCUSSION AND REFLECTION

1. Do you know any teenagers who are the primary caregivers for elders? How does this responsibility impact their school and social commitments?

2. What relationship did you have with your grandparents?

3. Samuel offers Eli nurture and Eli offers Samuel wisdom. How does this relate to Kira and Gran or to your own experience?

4. How can teenagers in church settings be connected to older people living alone?

5. Do you have teens and older adults in your family? Can they relate more effectively to one another?

ASSIGNMENT: Record It Verbatim

Gran and Kira's story is told in their own words rather than as a narrative. Focus on a conversation you've had in the last twenty-four hours with someone with whom you live. (Use a "typical" rather than a momentous situation.) Try to write it as dialogue—not little speeches, but the short fragments of normal conversation. Let imagination fill in the memory gaps. It may be longer than you anticipated once you write it down. Read it over and reflect on what you learn from "hearing" yourself on paper.

PRAYER

God, we pray for grandparents who are responsible for grandchildren and grandchildren who are responsible for grandparents. Ease the petty irritations of sharp tongues and loud music, of missed activities and cell phone waiting. Magnify the unexpected pleasures of nostalgic stories and shared television, of cookies and creativity. May love be the bridge across generations. Amen.

24   How Sharper Than a Serpent's Tooth

Genesis 9:18–28

The woman looked back at me with hollow eyes. Not an unusual story. Legally and ethically, Amanda DeMairs was an abuser and, now that her mother-in-law had died, remorse was eating away at her.

Amanda's mother-in-law had been a domineering woman who had raised her three children with harsh "religious" corporal punishment and a complete lack of appreciation for any of their gifts. David and Deborah were civil and remote, but Daniel had taken her in when arthritis and dementia had made independent living impossible. Daniel had had extensive therapy in his forties, working through his issues with his mother and his absent-all-the-time Dad. I know—I was his therapist, and he came to see me before taking her in. I concurred that he was able to distance the tyrant of his childhood from the vulnerable old woman. Of course, Daniel didn't have to stay home with her all day. The experiment with geriatric daycare was just that—an experiment. After three weeks Mrs. DeMairs "won"—she came home.

Amanda knew what kind of woman her mother-in-law was, and there was some underlying resentment on behalf of her husband and his siblings. Then there was common stress and exhaustion. In old age, Mrs. DeMairs whined. She called for little things—a glass of water, changing the television channel (since she didn't really understand the remote), finding her romance novel, her sweater, her slippers. Amanda clocked an average of four bells an hour—more when her mother-in-law knew she was on the telephone, transcribing tapes in her home office, or trying to fix dinner.

So the first abuse was neglect—ignoring the bells . . . only a couple times a day at first, then more frequently. The guilty woman sitting across from me sighed. "I guess I told myself I was just modifying her behavior, so she would combine her needs or . . ." Her voice drifted off then picked up again. "I always, always went to her at night. I didn't put her in danger. I just didn't answer all those unnecessary calls that meant she just wanted to boss someone around . . . or she was lonely." A couple times Mrs. DeMairs wet herself and Amanda felt terrible.

As the dementia progressed, Amanda had less free time. The kids studied at friends' homes and Daniel seemed to work late or go to church meetings more frequently than in the past. Amanda had to resign from the Diaconate. She gave up her gym membership—why pay for nothing? She couldn't remember when she had last gone to her quilting group. And, as the dementia progressed, Mrs. DeMairs became verbally unpleasant.

Friends came over and everything was going well. Mrs. DeMairs had been vulgar and nasty at dinner but Dan and Mandy's friends understood. After Amanda settled the older woman in bed, she thought they could play Trivial Pursuit or Balderdash. The fourth time Mrs. DeMairs called her to fix those "pesky pillows," Amanda went right up to her face and said, "If you ring that bell again, I'll pinch you."

The threat worked the first two times. "Then I had to pinch her. I just had to pinch her. And you know how easily old people bruise? The next morning I couldn't believe it. I was so good to her . . . I was like a slave for a week. But then it got to me again. And I did it again. And . . . I didn't feel so bad. I started being sure I didn't pinch her before a doctor's appointment. When Dan volunteered to dress her, I said that a woman's touch was better. I was hiding it from him!"

I asked her how many times a day she pinched her mother-in-law. Amanda looked at me with a horrified expression. "Not every day! Maybe once a week. God forgive me, I threatened her all the time. She'd be OK. Then she'd forget. I'd pinch her . . . just a little one. Listen to me!" She buried her face in her hands.

I wanted to feel sorry for her, but I really felt sorry for the tormented, confused old woman. If she were still living, I would have reported the abuse. But Mrs. DeMairs died a year ago and her death had nothing to do with pinches, neglect, or threats. My patient was sitting across from me crying.

In Mrs. DeMairs' religious community someone might say she reaped what she sowed. But not in Amanda and Daniel's mainline church. Should I tell Mandy to forgive herself? To tell her husband? To pay back by volunteering somewhere . . . not with confused elders?

I was curious. "Why did you make this appointment?"

"You'll think I'm crazy."

I didn't say anything.

"We went last week to the University Theatre. King Lear. I started to cry and I couldn't stop."

PSYCHOLOGICAL COMMENT

Elder abuse is a serious problem in our society. Often, when we think of "abusers," we picture mean, sadistic persons who feel powerful hurting others. Usually, this is not the case. Given the right circumstances every one of us can become an abuser. Feeling invulnerable to pressure or embarrassed about admitting the need for help are dangerous things.

The emotion of shame often underlies the abuse. When people feel shame, they isolate from others. This isolation increases the shame and makes it harder to get help. The increased shame creates anger, which can turn to rage. The rage explodes into abuse. Sadly, this creates more shame and the cycle continues. This story is a clear example of someone acting out her rage and shame, rather than seeking help. Amanda's frustrations are understandable and acceptable; however, her abusive behavior is not.

Abusive behavior often runs through multiple generations in families. Couples and families should talk with one another about their experiences and learn to manage their emotions healthfully in order to break the cycle. Dysfunctional patterns can be healed, but not without help.

BIBLICAL BACKGROUND

It is difficult to find biblical stories that reflect direct familial elder abuse. This passage, with its history of misuse as an excuse for African slavery, is presented as a situation of elder abuse. In the post-Flood, post-rainbow settlement, Noah planted a vineyard and became drunk. His third son Ham remarked on his father's nakedness, while the two older brothers averted their eyes and covered him. Apparently, not only direct cruelty but dishonor to the old brings a curse on the person who does it.

Similar stories filled with ambiguity include the tricking of Lot by his daughters (Gen. 37:29–30) and the lies of ten of Jacob's sons to him about their brother Joseph (Gen. 37), although Jacob's tricking of Isaac (Gen. 27) and Tamar's tricking of Judah (Gen. 38) seem justified by the text. The biblical witness, like contemporary experience, is filled with complex relationships.

QUESTIONS FOR DISCUSSION AND REFLECTION

1. Have you experienced, witnessed, or perpetrated abusive words or behaviors toward elders? Have you ever felt yourself slipping closer toward abuse of an elder (or a child or an animal)?

2. Elder abuse is rampant in our society. Do you think stricter laws and greater penalties will improve the situation?

3. Do you think an open discussion of the ambiguities of elder abuse would encourage people to get help?

4. In the biblical context an attitude of dishonor is considered abuse. Do you agree? Is there a hierarchy of attitude, neglect, and mental, verbal, and physical abuse—or are they all equally wrong?

5. Now that Daniel's mother has died, what steps toward healing might be possible for the children and inlaws?

ASSIGNMENT: Stick to It

This week (ignoring the groans of people who live with you) tape up some little messages. Some of them can be simple—"You are loved" on every mirror in the house; "Do you really want to eat it?"

on the refrigerator; "Enjoy every minute" on a clock; "Take a deep breath" on the door of someone you care for who is a) under two, b) over seventy, c) between eleven and eighteen. Engage the creativity of others in coming up with new messages and places to stick them. Take them down after a week so they don't get bedraggled. When you have forgotten, put them up again.

PRAYER

God of infinite patience, love, and gentleness, who absorbs our frustrations, fears, and petty feelings: forgive the hurt we have done and the kindness we have neglected, forgive the turmoil of angry thoughts, even the justified ones, forgive our failures to get help for ourselves or our failure to report others who should be reported. Lend your grace to situations of borderline mistreatment. Bless lawmakers, medical caregivers, and police as they respond to elder abuse. Comfort all those who fear their relatives this day. Amen.

25 ᕫ How Like Precious Oil

Psalm 133

You'll gain weight!" My hand pauses with a chunk of delicious Italian bread inches from the pool of olive oil swimming with basil. I wrinkle my nose at Karen and dip, soak, and pop the bread into my mouth and chew, deliberately licking my fingers.

"I'm going to enjoy every crumb. Actually I'm figuring the points this way—oil on my bread and balsamic vinegar on my lettuce. Voila—salad dressing!"

"You're in a good mood."

"You're grinning yourself."

"It's girls' night out. What's not to grin at, girl?" She beheads shrimp cocktail with relish. That's us—different flavor, same savor. The joking bounces back and forth until the main course comes and we can really "dish." Second and fourth Tuesdays every month for almost four years now, Karen and I go out to dinner. We never miss. Sometimes we've been joined by others. Every once in a while there's an emergency, but we'd rather change the menu than miss the meal and, although the hospital cafeteria doesn't have the same menu as our favorite Rubino's, it's open all hours.

The hospital is the kind of emergency we're likely to have.

Women get together for lots of reasons—some are work colleagues, sports or music boosters of their children's schools, empty nesters. Others are lonelyhearts from death or divorce, old high school friends, new breast cancer survivors. All those things connect and reconnect people, especially women.

Karen and I met in a waiting room. Her mom and my dad had neurology appointments. I saw her again at a dentist who catered to elders in wheelchairs. One look at each other and we *knew*. It was my idea—"I'm tired of being the sandwich generation. At least we can go out for real food!"

It took a while to coordinate the first date, but then we were hooked. We joke about lots of things, but we always share what's going on with our folks and how we feel about it. Karen left her position at the university and her own apartment to move in with her parents. She teaches one night at community college and tutors a couple of high school students. Divorced, she has a healthy dating life.

Thanks to me. I suggested that, if she had her parents 24/7, she could certainly afford some elder sitting. Now she even goes on the occasional vacation. Of course, she has a standing order for every other Tuesday. We brainstorm other things. How do you take the car keys away? How do you figure out Medicare D? How do you kill a brother who wants to go to his daughter's college Parents' Weekend, which falls on the folks' sixtieth wedding anniversary? (The solution is—change the date. If they both have some dementia, who's to know? Everybody came, no one was resentful, and the sweethearts had the best time at that wild faux-Hawaiian restaurant since their honeymoon.)

Karen helps me too—more than being my calamari conscience. "Jeannine," she said, "move them. Get them out of that monstrosity of a house and into a studio apartment in a facility with lots of care options. You *don't* have to bring them home to love them. They don't want it, Pete doesn't want it, you don't want it, and you're going to spend a lot more quality time with them if everyone can go home."

I found the Cedars and we've gone through three levels of care. It costs a lot and we'll go through all their money someday. We were really nervous about the finances last year but then my dad died of cancer in the summer. We spend so much time at the Cedars it seems like I should draw a salary for calling bingo, wheeling people to dinner, even feeding lonely old Fred.

It hasn't been all wonderful. After a change of directors, the Cedars hemorrhaged staff. Residents left in droves. The thought of moving my folks again seemed daunting. I dished a lot on Tuesday nights while visiting new places, then . . . things got better at the Cedars and worse for my dad.

Karen helped me through that and I helped her when she put her mom in a nursing home. Physically, neither she nor her dad could control Mama Beth, but Mama Beth cried and then died within twenty-four hours. Karen was left with the guilt. "One more day. I could have taken care of her one more day!" But she got through it. She's working a little more now and her dad is thriving three days a week at a wonderful geriatric daycare center.

Antipasto and love and friendship—we've been through a lot, and of course, we've had support from others. Karen's rabbi was wonderful with Mama Beth's funeral. Some of Karen's family are understanding and some are selfish, hateful, and greedy. Welcome to my world too. How people from the same family can have such different values, I don't know! But you can't pick your family.

You *can* pick your friends.

"I'll have a decaf with skim milk." I say.

Karen rolls her eyes and orders a mudslide!

PSYCHOLOGICAL COMMENTARY

The experience of caring for elders when one is in midlife can feel overwhelming and isolating. Developmentally, midlife is a time of full productivity in career and family. Yet the demands that surround this productivity allow little space for rest and rejuvenation. Our society has very few built-in supports for individuals engaged in caregiving. Thus, persons often have to create their own support networks. The women in this story provide many significant functions for each other, ranging from healing laughter to shared reality checks. Engaging in these moments together helps each to engage more fully in the responsibilities that they bear, and to know the joy as well as the struggles of caregiving. Fun as "girls' night out" may seem, Karen and Jeannine display enormous discipline in making this self-care commitment a priority.

BIBLICAL BACKGROUND

Psalms 120 through 134 are called Psalms of Ascent. They were worship songs, short and easy to memorize, which were used for travel to the three annual festivals that all Israelite men and most women attended. People traveled together through the dangerous terrain and the trip was made pleasant by singing songs together. (Psalm 134 actually appears to be a blessing for the return home.) Since Jerusalem is hilly and the Temple was located on Mount Zion, the journey involved "going up" or "ascending." However, Mt. Hermon, which is used poetically in the psalm, is the tallest mountain in Syria and is not near Jerusalem. It must have been the "hometown mountain" of the writer of the psalm.

The text reflects the practice of anointing in the ordination of priests (symbolized by Aaron, the first priest) mentioned in Exodus 29:7 as the epitome of joy. It may also refer to Deuteronomy 25:5, which calls for brothers to reside together so that, if one brother dies, the other can marry his widow and she does not need to marry a stranger. This custom of levirate marriage involved the ritual with the sandal dramatically portrayed in the book of Ruth. A more common contemporary biblical translation is "relatives" or "kindred" as those who dwell together in peace. Many of the Bible's stories testify to how rarely family harmony was achieved and how highly it was desired. In our day "kindred" may well be friends who *become* family and, indeed, we may ascend to share worship in each other's traditions.

QUESTIONS FOR DISCUSSION AND REFLECTION

1. What formal support systems are in your life—church, therapy, social workers, doctors, lawyers, household or medical assistance, senior centers, care planners, financial advisors, support groups? Which ones would you recommend to others?

2. What informal supports have you chosen for yourself and how do you nurture those relationships? Are some family and some friends?

3. The situation surrounding the death of Karen's mother would throw many people into suicidal depression. Have you ever had all your good work and planning go up in smoke? How did you respond?

4. There are one hundred and fifty psalms—one for every mood a person can feel. What psalm would you pray today?

ASSIGNMENT: Find Those Friends

Identify five friends—one you've known for a long time, one you've met recently, one who is a generation older than you, one younger person, and someone who is going through the same kind of life stage you are. Relatives don't count! If you can't think of someone in one of these categories, make a plan to make a new friend. For each friend you can identify, think about a way to nurture, support, or reengage that relationship—for the sake of your own emotional health and the health of anyone for whom you are caring.

PRAYER

God, for all the saints (and not so saintly ones), who have made different choices than ours but are always there for us—we give you thanks. For all the saints (and not so saintly ones), who are growing older and need us to be happy helping them to live the best life possible—we give you thanks. For all the saints (and not so saintly ones), who are our spouses and partners, siblings and children with their own needs—we give you thanks. For all the saints (and not so saintly ones), who are care managers, therapists, pastors, counselors, doctors, sponsors, hospice workers, funeral directors—professional all the way to the bottoms of their warm hearts—we give you thanks. And for you, O God, what a friend we have, what a friend we have in you. Amen

part seven

Caregiving — A Psychological and Spiritual Framework

Old men and old women shall again sit in the streets of Jerusalem, each with a staff in hand because of their great age.

ZECHARAH 8:4

26   Your People Shall Be My People
Emotional and Relational Truths of Caregiving

Leanne McCall Tigert

It is a gray Thursday afternoon in November as I sit in my pastoral psychotherapy office trying to focus my full attention on the midlife woman sitting across from me. She has come seeking support, advice, and a place to be still for one hour, while someone else listens. She has recently placed her father in a nursing home nearby. Most afternoons she leaves work and drives to her parents' house to pick up her mother and take her to the nursing home for a visit. Sometimes she brings her mother to her own house for dinner with the family afterwards. Then she drives her back to her house while the children do homework or play on the computer. She always walks her mom inside the back door, crossing over thresholds of memories and changes. She is sure to turn the lights on and the heat up, helping her mother to get settled before she leaves to do the same settling with her own children. She is exhausted and discouraged. Through tearful eyes, she speaks softly, "There are no good options. Dad will pass away soon. Mom doesn't want to move, but needs me to help her stay in her home. Honestly, moving her would require even more work for me. My kids are good. They understand, but it wears on them. Besides, I'm missing out on time with them, and I know they need me around more. Sometimes they get pretty cranky about it. Who can blame them? I'm so tired. I can't keep up."

I feel discouraged listening to her. She is right—there are no good, simple, pain-free options. I know that from my clients' lives as well as my own. As I sit with clients I am aware of the demands of my own life—two parents with chronic health problems and two teenagers trying to make their way in the world, each of whom needs help and attention.

If this were true only of a few clients and myself, I would think we were down on our luck. However, I hear some version of this scenario every day—with friends, colleagues, clients, parishioners, and students. The case studies that have been included in this book are representative of some of the situations, but by no means all of them. Although the exact numbers are difficult to know, experts agree that there are more elderly now than ever, and there are increasing numbers of family members caring for them. In the United States today, more than thirty-three million people are caring for someone fifty years or older. It is estimated that family members provide about 80 percent of care for the elderly. Usually, women devote 50 percent more time to this than men, and often one person serves as the primary caregiver, with help from other family members. Approximately half of care recipients still live in their own homes, with 20 to 25 percent living with their caregivers. About 4 percent are in assisted living facilities, and 5 percent are in nursing homes. African Americans and Hispanics are much more likely to live in multigenerational households than are European Americans. In 1998 there were thirty-five million persons over the age of sixty-five (13 percent of the population). In 2035, it is projected that there will be more than seventy million (over 20 percent) in this age range.[1]

As more people live longer with chronic physical illnesses and disabilities, rates of depression, substance abuse, and emotional distress are also increasing. Some of this is related to the increase in the incidence of Alzheimer's disease (up from four million to a projected fourteen million), while much is due to attempts to cope with dependency and loss of meaning, purpose, and value in life.[2]

How do we manage caring for our elders and our children, while caring for ourselves? Is it possible not only to manage caregiving, but to grow and experience fulfillment and joy in giving care to an elder? In a society that values independence and youth over community and wisdom, the stresses and strains of caregiving have reached epidemic proportions. The psychological, emotional, and spiritual costs can be high for everyone involved. Yet, there are also significant joys. Families are resilient. Siblings, children, friends, and neighbors find new meaning and connections while caring for those they love. I have spoken more with my brothers in the past year than in the previous decade, and the new bond may carry us beyond this stage in our lives. I have heard many others describe similar experiences, sometimes with surprise, but almost always with gratitude.

Individuals often find an inner strength and a core faith that they thought was missing. People are remarkable and, more often than not, find themselves making choices from deep within to care for and love others as fully as possible. So, whether one finds oneself on the newly labeled "daughter–track" (the experience of leaving one's career to care at home for one's parents), adjusting one's business travel to accommodate a trip to the retirement center, or involved in weekly updates with one's siblings, he or she is not alone.

There are common psychological themes expressed by the stories shared here and many others. Each individual experiences a particular variation of the realities of loss, change, limits, and letting go. Everyone is forced into making choices about how to respond to each other's needs, wants, and expectations. Everyone must face oneself, prioritizing what and who is important. Finally, each one is thrust into those questions of ultimate importance about the understanding and experience of God, love, life, and death.

Perhaps the most significant overarching theme in this experience is that of loss. It has been said that people begin to know loss from the moment they are born. Indeed, every day that passes is lost. However, until the time of later midlife, most people are focused on growing, increasing, dreaming, gaining. Losses become a part of our larger gains. For example, a person loses baby teeth but gains adult teeth or leaves college to begin a career. In midlife, people begin to experience losses that are irreplaceable. As elders become infirm and need care, adult children must grieve the loss of active parent figures in their lives. In order to "parent the parents," one must let go of illusions that Dad or Mom is going to be there to fix everything. This kind of caregiving requires both the children and parents to let go of their previous roles with one another, yet remain respectful of the past. Often when I am helping my mother dress, I experience an unexplainable sadness welling up inside of me. Sometimes it makes me want to run out of the room. Then I realize that I'm missing the mother who used to help me get dressed, and that our roles have shifted forever. There is no going back. Yet she is still my mother and my elder who needs to be treated with dignity and respect, as well as tenderness.

Many of my clients speak about the unanticipated anxiety brought on by the death of a parent. "It's like there is nothing between me and the great beyond. Who is going to stand between me and God?" someone once said in my office. Elders act as a kind of spiritual buffer against death and eternity. Perhaps this explains why some adult children have such a difficult time letting go of parents. It can be very scary to be the most grown-up, the next to become old, and, perhaps, the next to die.

Aging itself is a daily experience of loss. Some of these losses are obvious to all, while others are smaller and unseen. In the book *Losses in Later Life*, R. Scott Sullender writes, "Losses also become cumulative in nature after age forty. Losses build upon losses, and in a sense foreshadow the ultimate loss of life itself. . . .we need to understand the particular losses of the second half of life and how to deal with them in ways that augment our emotional and spiritual health." He goes on to name seven losses of particular significance: loss of youth, loss of family, loss of parents, loss of work, loss of one's spouse/partner, loss of health, and the loss of identity.[3] One time I suggested to my father that he go out and have lunch with his buddies. He looked at me and said, "You know, the guys I used to have working lunches with are dead." Another time, he turned to me to help him open up a jar of pickles. He wasn't able to turn the top. Loss is a daily experience that builds into a process for which we are rarely prepared.

Another common theme of this time concerns generational differences in worldview, experience, and skills. Mary Pipher writes about this in her book *Another Country: Navigating the Emotional Terrain of Our Elders*. Baby boomers and our parents have a very different emotional makeup. Those currently older than seventy were raised in the time of the Great Depression and World War II. Their children were raised in the era of modern psychology, emotional process, and drastically changing roles of men and women. Pipher describes "time-zone issues," meaning that our differing generations have very different ideas about ways to communicate and to handle stress. "When we talk with people of other generations, we often experience very real differences in style and tone. Our parents grew up in a world in which the word "consumption" referred to tuberculosis, and depression was not a mental health problem but an era of economic disaster. . . . It is important to remember that our differences are not pathological, characterological, or personal; they are generational."[4]

I often remind myself that both of my parents were deeply affected by the Depression, the premature death of my father's father, and the permanent disability of my mother's father. Each of these events occurred before the time of Social Security disability or death benefits. People learned to do what needed to be done and not spend much time talking about it. When I ask them to tell me how they feel about something, they may look at me like I am speaking another language, or they tell me what needs to be done. When I remember their culture, I try to ask it a different way. My father keeps a copy of Mary Pipher's book by his bedside. He says that it helps him understand himself.

Another significant loss experienced in this stage of life is that of the loss of identity. This is more obvious with the elderly and infirm than it is with their younger caregivers; however, it is true of both. As one ages, he or she is forced to let go of physical strength and health, career, peers who have died, home, the ability to drive at night (and then to drive at all), among numerous other skills that are often taken for granted. Each time this happens, people may experience a kind of mini identity crisis, asking themselves, "Who am I now that I can't drive my wife out to dinner?" or "Who am I now that my best friends are all gone?"

Similarly, caregiving in midlife also requires a renegotiation of one's sense of self. Suddenly, one begins balancing medication regimens instead of ledger sheets, and organizing trips to multiple medical offices rather than interoffice business meetings. "Who am I when I visit with my friends and all I'm thinking about is whether Mom has enough Depends to get through the day?" The more involved we are, the more the person we know ourselves to be changes.

Each of these experiences of loss, change, and renegotiation can sometimes feel overwhelming, but none has to be insurmountable. They are each part of the puzzle of being human. As such, they are all opportunities for rich spiritual growth and discernment. In the process of aging, most people tend to recognize that it is the spiritual truths that ground life in the experience of so much change and grief. As people ask, "Who am I?" in the midst of letting go, they come upon one answer that does not change. "I am a beloved child of God, no matter what else I must let go of." Prayer, meditation, and connection with God witness to the only "love that will not let me go."

Although the particulars are different for midlife caregivers, the foundation of faith and spiritual growth is essential. Caregivers often feel overwhelmed and powerless in the midst of so much need. Midlife baby boomers have been raised to think they—we—can accomplish most anything. After all, when we were young, astronauts landed on the moon, and to many of us it was no big deal, even though our elders could not believe it. Caregiving for our elders places us squarely in front of a normative spiritual crisis. We discover that we are not limitless and all-powerful. We cannot accomplish everything we want to. We cannot fix everything. We are not God. Caregiving opens the door to moving away from complete self-reliance to healthy reliance on God. In the experience of turning over to God through prayer and meditation all that is out of human control and ability, midlifers can build a truly profound faith that will carry them through their own future renegotiations and changes in life. To trust in God rather than our own self-reliance allows us to fully enter the experience of loving and caring for someone else, for we know that even as we let go, we are never truly alone.

The dynamics of this stage of life are many, complex, and ever changing for everyone. To care for another human being is sacred work. To be cared for is to know vulnerability and grace. Both bind us intimately to one another. My own family has struggled for more than four years with the declining health of my parents. Before that, my mother and father cared for their parents and an elderly aunt. My partner's family is constantly on the phone and computer, sharing the work of caring for the family's eldest. I am learning over time that there is something hopeful and redemptive being handed down through the generations. It is not always functional. It is rarely easy. But it is the essence of what it means to be human. There is a saying in the United Church of Christ: To believe is to care; to care is to do." In your believing, caring, and doing, may you know love.

NOTES

1. Hugh Delehanty and Elinor Ginzler, *Caring for Your Parents: The Complete AARP Guide* (New York: Sterling Publishing, 2005) 13, 14.

2. Harold Koenig, "Pastoral Counseling with the Aged," *Clinical Handbook of Pastoral Counseling*, vol. 3, ed. Robert J. Wicks, Richard D. Parsons, and Donald Capps (New York: Paulist Press, 2003), 38.

3. R. Scott Sullender, *Losses in Later Life* (New York: Paulist Press, 1989), 3.

4. Mary Pipher in Delehanty and Ginzler, *Caring for Your Parents*, xiv.

Your God Shall Be My God

The Scriptures That Question Our Answers—
Spiritual Dimensions of Caregiving

Maren C. Tirabassi

During one of his many hospitalizations, my father was given a drug that increased the delusions associated with the dementia of his Alzheimer's disease. He could vividly see himself dueling with the Devil using his grandfather's Civil War saber. He would strike the Devil a savage blow and Satan would be shattered into little "devilettes." They would coalesce and Russell would start fighting again. He told me he knew that when the Devil won, he'd die. Russell was still in a stage when he could laugh at this waking dream in a way that he could not laugh at the sleeping nightmares that replayed Dachau prison camp or the lynching he witnessed from high up in a tree when he was a little boy.

Death was the Devil was the Enemy. This equation made hospice hard for Russell when the time came and he could have benefited from its gentle care. It came from a place deep in his religious consciousness and it caused him to battle death bitterly until the very end of his life. He was appalled by the behavior of residents who chose to stop eating in the facility where he lived. He said, "I'll always be a fighter."

Russell's premise was based on what he thought should be in the Bible. Death is bad—life is good. Avoiding death at all costs is being a good Christian. Unfortunately, our faith, like our lives . . . and our deaths . . . is much more ambivalent. First Corinthians 15 assures us that death has lost its sting and that the physical disintegration of a human body is not a victory for evil but the passing of a temporary shape, a bare seed, in which we experience the blessing of creation and anticipate a spiritual body. Second Corinthians 5:4 suggests that it is valid and faithful to long for death, to groan for our mortality to be swallowed by true "life."

There are as many interpretations of what happened on Calvary and at the empty tomb as there are interpreters. The nature of atonement is a confusing concept. It is clear, however, that Jesus did not fight his own death. He went forward to meet it. A tenet of faith, variously interpreted, discussed, and described by pearly gates or tunnels of light, is that in some way we cannot know until we do know—Jesus' crucifixion and resurrection change everything. Death itself need no longer be feared. Believing this alters how we anticipate our own mortality and how we care for those whose frailty makes it likely that death is their next great challenge.

A multitude of resources for people who are making decisions about the aging issues of family members give practical and sometimes psychological advice. As the "baby boom" becomes the "sandwich generation," creative solutions for managing aging have expanded and there's literature about residential options, medical support, financial strategy. However, people in our churches are drowning in helpful web sites without a raft for their spiritual concerns. Some questions are specific—What does number "five" of the Ten Commandments mean in light of the man who walked out on my mother and me? Why do I feel like the older brother in the prodigal son story, compelled to share *my* half of the legacy and scolded for a lack of joy? How do I reconcile Jesus' statement "let the dead bury the dead" with his criticism of the "*corban* scam?" How did Ruth and Boaz really feel when Naomi called Obed *her* child? Ultimately we are asking: what does our faith say about the issues we are facing?

These and other biblical passages have been highlighted in the preceding stories. Scripture echoes our questions and offers guidance to our situations. There are, however, two overarching themes that emerge from multiple passages throughout the biblical text. These themes (like the issue of "death-as-enemy") may seem counterintuitive or frankly disturbing, if we expect the text to shore up what we already think of as good "family values."

Many of us are distressed by the blatant "youth worship" of our culture and would like to celebrate the amazing gifts of older people. However, our tradition is not one that reveres and cares for elders in the same way that many Asian and Native American traditions do. Jesus of Nazareth was a *young* man who directly refuted the assumption that older heads were wiser. (John 8:57–58) Not only this confrontation story, but the single anecdote from his childhood (Jesus staying behind in the Temple) suggests that youth has much to offer to those older. Jesus did not surround himself with sage advisors, but with hot-headed disciples of his own generation.

Older people in the Bible are frequently portrayed not as wise, but as foolish and vulnerable. Isaac is tricked by his son Jacob who himself in his old age divides his family by blatant favoritism. Eli, the old high priest, is badgered by his biological sons and advised by his adoptive grandson. David, as an old king, loses his keen judgment, and Nicodemus, the old and esteemed teacher, comes timidly in the night to visit Jesus and then betrays a basic lack of understanding.

Balancing these major protagonists are some minor older players—Melchizedek, who blesses Abraham; Jethro, who advises his son-in-law Moses; Simeon and Anna, who recognize Jesus as the Messiah. Also there are certainly examples of cooperation across the generations. Mordecai has wisdom and Esther has a plan; Naomi has a plan and Ruth the courage to carry it out; Jeremiah, who was called into prophecy at an incredibly young age, in his old age turns to Baruch to preserve his insight.

There is no denying, however, that the Bible portrays elders who whine, make mistakes, and are demanding, intolerant, and lonely as often or more often than elders who offer challenge and give love. Far from the platitude to "care for your dear sweet old Mum and Dad who have done everything for you," the Bible offers a realistic picture of complex relationships between the generations with a slight bias toward the wisdom and leadership of youth. This does not seem very comforting to us as we seek meaning in our caregiving for elders in a "throwaway" society.

In the book of the prophet Joel are these famous words:

Then afterward I will pour out my spirit on all flesh;
your sons and your daughters shall prophesy,
your old men shall dream dreams,
and your young men shall see visions.

Even on the male and female slaves,
  in those days, I will pour out my spirit. (Joel 2:28–29)

Peter repeats Joel's prophecy on Pentecost morning to describe what is happening as the gospel reaches out in many languages. The Spirit of God lights up people of all ages. The young are not the only ones with fresh inspiration nor are the old the distinctive repository of "I told you so." The biblical witness shows people of every age, gender, and economic status with wisdom appropriate to their own experiences. None is discarded or disregarded.

Beyond even this text I would claim that the Spirit rests even on people with memory loss, the most vulnerable in our society because they have lost even that which identifies the self as the self and speak in "tongues" that only God understands. They, indeed, may be the ones put down in our contemporary midst of which we hear, "unless you become like a child . . ." you shall not enter the community of God.

Not only does the biblical text not sugarcoat elders as "the wise," it is not nearly as "family friendly" as many of us wish it were. The central code of the Torah, the Ten Commandments, contains an injunction to honor one's parents. It certainly must not be a natural human urge if it needs a commandment. It is noteworthy as well that it does not contain any language about *loving* parents.

The Gospels show Jesus of Nazareth quoting what was scripture for him, the Pentateuch, to name his "greatest" commandments with *love* as the verb—love of God and love of neighbor. He invites his followers to love one another and challenges them to love their enemies . . . but he never asks them to love their parents. Even more disturbing to our eldercare agenda is how Jesus redefines family away from a biological relationship and toward a chosen community of collegial work and mutual care. When his mother and siblings come to remonstrate with him, he claims that his followers are all the family he needs. He denies a would-be disciple's request to bury a parent or even say good-bye to people at home. He suggests that a life of faith will drive a wedge between parents and children, siblings one with another, in-laws. Does he have to be so right?

The New Testament does have a few tender moments between the generations. Jesus heals his disciple Peter's mother-in-law and he raises from death the son of a widow from Nain who has no one else to care for her. Paul of Tarsus, who describes his ancestors but never his family, asks Philemon, the slave owner, for the manumission of the Onesimus so that the young man may care for Paul in his frail health. There is, however, no injunction for a younger person to forego the life stage of creativity and generativity to assist a parent or grandparent, and there are many biblical passages that devalue family ties and encourage what appears to be selfish independence in the name of following Christ. Most pastors avoid preaching from these texts, although faith communities that demand a high level of commitment use them to separate college-age converts from their parents and siblings. Mainline denominations often identify such groups as sects or cults.

The passages themselves are there! The New Testament does not insist on any family loyalty. "Let the dead bury the dead," resolves most eldercare dilemmas. Fortunately for the community of faith, and unfortunately for anyone who depends on these scriptures to escape obligation, we discover that underlying them there is a challenge to even deeper responsibility. Christian caregiving does not parallel family ties but expands them to a universal compassion. The fourth gospel remembers that Jesus on the cross gave responsibility to care for his mother, Mary, to his disciple John.

Jesus' community, which he called family, embraced men and women, the rich and the poor, the educated and the uneducated, and he spoke to that community about the importance of the single lost sheep, the dust-covered coin. He told a story about a prodigal *father* who donated a portion of his older son's legacy to his impecunious younger son's fiesta and yet was worthy to be loved by both children. In his last words to his disciples in the gospel of John, Jesus used the ultimate family image, "I will not leave you *orphaned*, I am coming to you" (John 14:18). No one—*no one*—is orphaned; *no one* is childless. The early Christian community was defined in Acts by the provision of all needs from mutually held wealth (Acts 2:44). The first deacons were established to care for all widows . . . whether they had children or not (Acts 6:1–6).

I expressed my condolences to a woman I know from the assisted care facility where at one time or another six of my older relatives were living. She, too, visited several, and this was the occasion of her final loss. "Well, one good thing," she said, "I'm finished now and I can get on with my life."

Listening to Jesus of Nazareth, I don't think a day like that will ever come for me. I'll look around me—here are my mother and my father, my sister and my brothers, all of these, including the lonely Jewish woman with Parkinson's disease waiting for her husband and dog to come take her for a walk and the cranky man who's alienated his children so severely they don't even visit on holidays. They are my family.

Perhaps the reason that Jesus doesn't let the would-be disciple, or us, say good-bye to the "home folks" is that we can never go to a place where someone doesn't need our attention, where we are not in the midst of *family*. In contemporary times the shapes of our families are undergoing radical change. Families are extended and blended, chosen as well as born. Scripturally speaking, this is not a problem. It is as true to biblical family values as it can be in a society so unsupportive of the medical and social needs of its most marginal members.

Zechariah offers a prophesy as wonderful as Joel's:

> Thus says the LORD of hosts: Old men and old women shall again sit in the streets of Jerusalem, each with staff in hand because of their great age. And the streets of the city shall be full of boys and girls playing in its streets . . . For there shall be a sowing of peace; the vine shall yield its fruit, the ground shall give its produce, and the skies shall give their dew; and I will cause the remnant of this people to possess all these things. (Zech. 8:4–5, 12)

Death is not the enemy. Elders are neither wiser nor more foolish than the rest of us—but just as gifted, as blessed, as precious in God's eyes. The biological family is not the biblically sanctified caregiving unit, though radical compassion and tenderness for all may well *begin* in the crucible of the needs and concerns of those closest. Caregiving is an ongoing task and calling and joy for the entire community of faith—to the end that everyone hears these echoes from Mark, from Romans, from Matthew: here is my mother and my father and child . . . it is that very Spirit bearing witness with our spirit that we are the children of God . . . and if you have done it for the oldest of these you have done it for me.

This brief list provides a wealth of information; however, resources are constantly changing. An online search with the informed assistance of a pastor or eldercare professional may help you respond to particular concerns.

Delehanty, Hugh, and Elinor Ginzler. *Caring for Your Parents: The Complete AARP Guide.* New York: Sterling Publishing, 2005.

Erikson, Eric, Joan Erikson, and Helen Kivnick. *Vital Involvement in Old Age: The Experience of Old Age in Our Time.* New York: Norton, 1986.

Mace, Nancy L., and Peter V. Rabins. *The 36-Hour Day: A Family Guide to Caring for People with Alzheimer Disease, Other Dementias, and Memory Loss in Later Life.* Baltimore: Johns Hopkins University Press, 2001.

Pipher, Mary. *Another Country: Navigating the Emotional Terrain of Our Elders.* New York: Riverhead Books, 1999.

Strauss. Claudia J. *Talking to Alzheimer's: Simple Ways to Connect When You Visit with a Family Member or Friend.* Oakland, Calif.: New Harbinger Publications, 2001.

Sullender, R. Scott. *Losses in Later Life: A New Way of Walking with God.* New York: Paulist Press, 1989.

Wicks, Robert J., Richard D. Parsons, and Donald Capps, eds. *Clinical Handbook of Pastoral Counseling,* vol. 3. New York: Paulist Press, 2003.

www.caremanager.org (National Association of Professional Geriatric Care Managers)

www.growthhouse.org (resources of grieving)

www.healingenvironments.org (support for those who care for the dying)

www.AARP.org (American Association of Retired Persons)

www.NCOA.org (National Council on Aging)

scripture index

OLD TESTAMENT

NEW TESTAMENT

topic index